Mommy, When Will The Lord Be Two?

Mommy, When Will The Lord Be Two?

A CHILD'S EYE VIEW OF BEING JEWISH TODAY

RUTH SELIGMAN
and JONATHAN MARK

Introduction by
Rabbi Tsvi Blanchard

KENSINGTON BOOKS
http://www.kensingtonbooks.com

KENSINGTON BOOKS are published by

Kensington Publishing Corp.
850 Third Avenue
New York, NY 10022

ISBN 1-57566-470-4

First Printing: October, 1999
10 9 8 7 6 5 4 3 2 1

Printed in the United States of America

With love to our children
Sara Noa Nechama, Rivka Yona Moriah, and Zev
Mordechai, the most inspiring people on earth.

And to our mothers
Barbara Rosenbaum Seligman and Elaine Malina Mark,
and our fathers
Rabbi William Seligman and Dr. Mortimer Mark of blessed memory,
who all listened to their children.

ACKNOWLEDGMENTS

Thanks to Tracy Bernstein at Kensington Publishing Corp. for her idea and vision, and for her patient and enthusiastic editing. Thanks also to Gareth Esersky, our agent at the Carol Mann Agency, who makes all things seem possible in a lively way. Thanks to Yitta Halberstam-Mandelbaum, for her faith and limitless generosity. To our families—Adley Mandel and Susan Seligman Mandel, Micha, Mariel, Abba Zev and Yardena Mandel, whose inspiration is awesome and insights were the first noticed; Deborah Mark; Rabbi Tsvi Blanchard, Nomi Mark, Deena, Tali, Tamar, Elana and Elisheva Blanchard—we thank you for your ever available ears, your comments, and your encouragement. Thanks also to our amazing cousins everywhere. Very special thanks to Natalie Muhammed, for the gift of peace of mind. For their assistance, thanks to Devora Steinmetz, Gary Pretzfelder and the staff at Beit Rabban; Rabbi Manny Vinas; Carol Spivack and the staff of the Riverdale Temple Nursery School; Rabbi Joel Cohen; Rabbi Aaron Frank; Rabbi Richard Kirsch; Nurit Bacharach and the staff of Gan Miriam; Rina Cohen, Michele Singer and the schools of Congregation Rodeph Shalom; SAR Academy; the Hebrew Institute of Riverdale; Riverdale Jewish Center; The Riverdale Y; The JCC on the Hudson; The Conservative Synagogue of Riverdale; Chabad of New York; and the Mosholu-Montefiore Center. Very special thanks to Eve Yudelson at the Jewish Communication Network, David Rosenthal at Shamash.org, David and Rose Schwartz, Arnine Weiss, jump starters Irrit Dweck and Linda Botwinik; Susan Kaufman, Cantor Jerry Held, Alice Harvey Eigner, Sara Averick, Danny Siegel, Suzanne Popkin, Donna Green and Oona Goodman for their assistance over the Internet and over the miles—with special, special thanks to Sandra Lilienthal. For their support, thanks go to Chavi Diamond, Tzipporah Spear-Tyck, Ruth Weiss, and the staff of AIRUS! Publishing Group; and to Dr. Ruth Westheimer; Alan and Renee Leicht; Rita Rosencrantz; Patty Dann and Eric Nooter; Clara Mark, Jeanne and Raymond Kaufman, Lili Weiser, Zisu and Otto Weiss, Kuni and Breindu Rosenbaum, Zishe and Frieda Rosenbaum; Judith Leventhal; Nancy Miller; Leah Beth Ward, Michele Lesie, Carol Missler, Betsy O'Connell and Claire Ansberry; Shalini Dewan; Lisa Laden; Rickie Weiner; Cantor Joseph Gole; Charlene Grant; Frances Gozland; Andrea and Michael Pariser; Robert Simon; Stanley Davis; Miraim Holmes; Lee Gomes, Pam Mendels; Robin Schatz; Cherie Hart and John Bleho; Susan Hostetler and Lelai Lelaulu, who understand much about the spiritual life of children; Aviva Patz; Gia McKenzie; Marion Fishman; Debbie Jonas and gang; Susan Kantar; and Sandy Adelsberg for the right words; as well as to Ari Goldman, Shira Dicker, Sandee Brawarsky and greatly to Rachel Stern for their enthusiasm. Special thanks to Judy Schwartz for the gift of time and caring, and to Eliot, Rachel and Jenny Schwartz; and to Stephen Kaufman for his loyal support. Thanks for everything always go to David Gale, and to Marialisa Calta and Dirk Van Susteren and family for countless goodnesses way before Vermont.

Contents

Introduction

Jews have always been great commentators on both text and life. Jews are always asking questions about what somebody or something means. From the first rabbis, Jewish scholars have playfully looked through inherited texts in search of creative opportunities for surprising and even funny ways to understand the Bible, the Talmud and other classics of Jewish tradition. Jews of all walks of life, as well, love looking at books and life from uncommon angles. Jews love discovering unexpected meanings in ordinary places.

Children can definitely help us see things in new ways. Their unanticipated perspectives on the world can both entertain us and deepen our understanding. Listen to this story. Unaware of the stunning beauty of the day, a frazzled parent is rushing the children out to school in the morning. All of a sudden, one of the kids stops to thank God for a beautiful day! "You did it, Hashem. You did it! You made a beautiful day!" Everything is transformed. Now there is laughter. Now there is love. And beyond the inherent cuteness, there is an extraordinary chance for a delightful appreciation of the wonder and beauty of creation.

This little book, *Mommy, When Will the Lord Be Two?*, is a collection of holy sayings. Many of them open our eyes to the world of the spirit that children see. How can you listen to the voices of these children who are at once inspiring, awesome and even very funny? First, enjoy the laughter. Then I suggest that you may continue by imitating the Talmudic rabbi who uncovered a deeper meaning in his life by turning to the way schoolchildren read the Bible. Finally, don't miss the very special sacred moments that the spirit of children will surely bring you.

Rabbi Tsvi Blanchard, Ph.D.
Director of Organizational Development
at the National Jewish Center for Learning and
Leadership (CLAL)

Foreword

As told in the Torah, Abraham, Isaac and their servants walked to their legendary rendezvous with a ram on Mount Moriah, to the place that would one day be Jerusalem's Temple Mount in the heart of the heart of the country. On this day, there was no city, no shuk of a marketplace, no five-star hotels, no Temple—nothing but a wild terrain where rams would get their horns stuck in the bramble.

Abraham asked his adult servants what they saw.

"A mountain," said one.

"A dusty road," said another.

They told the truth. They were honest and well meaning.

Abraham asked the child Isaac. Isaac, befitting the Hebrew meaning of his name *Yitzhak*, laughed. The child looked at the hill and said he saw a Temple, then a second Temple and a third; he saw a city on the hill; he saw the end of the story, a place of happy endings, a Zion that would seem, to those who returned, "like a dream. Then our mouths will fill with laughter and our tongues with glad song."

Well now, thought Abraham. He left the others and walked on with the child alone.

For Abraham knew that a religion, a family, a people, could never be built or sustained by those whose wisdom was dry, literal and rational. It could only be kept alive by those whose minds were fluid and fanciful, by children who can see angels in the shadows, souls inside of bodies, honey in the rock.

At the cusp of a new millennium, the eyes of Jewish children are given a new task. Instead of Isaac seeing glory where adults see only a dusty hill, children today are presented with three thousand years of organized religion and history, and yet they can see clearly through to the essence, to the original delight. They can look at the spiritual and material architecture of Judaism and yet can imagine Eden. Taught the literal truth, they articulate a response that is nothing less than poetry and song.

Perhaps this is because they are only a few years removed from the company of angels and Heaven. In so many ways, they are as close to that world as to this one. In this world, children know all too well that they are strangers in a strange land, yet they are thrilled and amused by what they are discovering with every new day and holiday.

Where do babies come from? According to Jewish tradition, the answer to that question is not just biological but spiritual. Reb Nachman, prince of Breslov, told the legend of the world's wisest men, who were trying to remember the most ancient of all stories. One said he remembered when "the apple was cut from the branch," the cutting of the umbilical cord; another, "when the lantern was burning," as the fetus is said to learn the mysteries of Heaven from a faculty of angels while a lantern illuminates the womb. Yet another said he remembered when the fragrance entered the fruit, when the soul and spiritual imagination became as much a part of the baby as its softness.

This, said Reb Nachman, was the greatest, most ancient story of all. As long as there have been crisp autumn mornings and new school years, the essence of this story has been taught—a story that is almost subversive: that there is a spirit in the world that goes beyond ourselves; that God's children, with little fingers, have a story to tell; that there is such a thing as holiness; that children are holy, created in the image of God; that the seventh day is holier than the other six; that there is a calendar with seasons and holidays to unravel and to marvel at.

As far back as antiquity, and today in chasidic cheders and in suburban Reform temple nurseries, the story is remarkably the same. Whether in the Yeshiva of Shem and Ever in ancient Sfat, in the schools on Warsaw's Krachmalna Street, in Jewish nurseries within the Atlas Mountains of Morocco or on side streets in the Bronx, Jewish children feel that "all this" is theirs. Bible stories are not something distant but as close as a nursery rhyme, like God telling Noah:

> *There's going to be a floody, floody.*
> *Get those children out of the muddy, muddy, children of*
> *the Lord!*

Parents fear the world is more complicated than that. We wonder if we can build a Noah's ark of our own to protect our children from a world where indeed there are things more scary than witches and wolves and bad dreams. Perhaps there is no greater "ark" than the power of spiritual freedom and imagination, the power that comes from feeling intimate with things eternal. We try to keep that ark afloat, taking photographs and videos, writing down astounding truths from the mouths of babes as they sail away on the ark to tomorrow, the most ancient story of all.

In the end, we have our stories, both personal and bespeaking a larger peoplehood. Nearly eighty years ago, young Morty, returning from his first day of kindergarten at his Bronx public school, announced with surprise to his Yiddish-speaking parents: "*Mameh, Tateh*. My teacher speaks such a beautiful English." The story from that distant afternoon is still told by the children of that child who grew up to be a doctor in modern America. The story is told with laughter and affection, speaking volumes about a child's amazement at the ordinary world, as filtered through the Jewish immigrant experience.

Every family has such a nugget at the heart of its history, and the Jewish family collectively has inherited enough similar gems in our larger history, as well.

In *Mommy, When Will the Lord Be Two?*, we sought to capture and record children's views about being Jewish in the world today and their expressions of Jewishness. We uncovered dozens of nuggets of wonder, surprise, belief and perception that led to a deeper understanding of the Jewish experience and of how religion in general, and Judaism in particular, is transmitted to our children—indeed, how it is transmitted to the future at a time when Jewish continuity is a matter of deep concern.

Judaism is a religion rich in ritual, steeped in history, dictated by law, transmitted in a once-ancient language and binding over centuries often through community and family practice and tradition.

To some it's not an easy religion to follow, especially in this modern age, and Jewish leaders across the denominational spectrum often struggle with ways to make it "come alive." They might do well to listen to their children.

Children, in their ever discovering and discerning approach to the world, find in Judaism a context in which to set their own growth and growing up. We found this to be true in hundreds of interviews with Jewish children at synagogues, Jewish community centers and religious schools across the country, as well as across the denominational spectrum of Jewish observance. We posed basic questions about belief and observance and heard enthusiastic answers that often inspired deep discussion. We spoke to a dozen Sarahs and Saras, half a dozen Ariels and Ariellas, several Yardenas, (including the two-year-old who called herself "Mydana") and more than a few kids named Max, Rachel, Jonathan, Rebecca, Talia and Sam, as well as the Kaylas, Emmas, Samanthas and Bens, who claim the names popular among Jewish families today. The children had questions, too—questions that offered a sense of how they integrate a world of ritual, belief, mystery and history into the framework of their daily lives. Their answers and insights make up most of *Mommy, When Will the Lord Be Two?*

In the course of this project, we were rewarded with choice stories told by parents and teachers, and we'll share some of those, as well.

During our interviews, we learned several truths. Among these was the natural acceptance with which children approach belief. Imbued with awe over the miracles of biblical times, children are willing to appreciate miracles in their own lives. Karen, age 6, had a way of seeing ancient miracles transformed for modern purpose. "You know how God helped Pharaoh's daughter reach the basket with baby Moses floating in the Nile River by stretching out her arm? That's how God helps Michael Jordan get the ball in the basket. He stretches out Michael's arm."

Rebecca, age 2, who calls herself a "Hebrew," refers to God as "Hashem," as He is often called in nonliturgical conversation. Rebecca sees miracles in her everyday life, announcing in congratulatory tones, as she strides onto her doorstep at the start of her morning, "You did it, Hashem, You did it! You made a beautiful day!"

And Sarah, age 7, turned her classmates into silently nodding believers when she stated softly, "A miracle happened when we prayed for my baby brother to come out of the hospital when he was sick, and he did."

Another insight came from the way we found children able to incorporate the lessons of the Bible into their lives. Children learn of the feats of characters in the biblical narrative and are happy to place these characters on a plane with the superheroes of their own popular culture. Abraham teaches them about having the courage to stand up for what they believe; Moses teaches how to lead. So said dozens of children we met during these interviews.

Lessons were learned from the Ten Commandments, which give children a reason for good behavior. When asked, nearly every child listed "respect your parents, respect your teachers" at the top, and the context gave them the comfort to know they were doing the right thing.

We learned that, for children, the relationship with God is one of intimate identification. Thus, when four-year-old Sarah was taught by her parents to say the "Sh'ma"—the prayer that embodies the basic tenet of Judaism, "Hear O Israel, the Lord Our God, the Lord is One"—each night at bedtime, she felt intimate enough to ask, "Mommy, when will the Lord be two?"

Was she expressing her own year-round anticipation of her birthday and relating to God's? Better yet, she simply and already thought of God not as a distant, bearded, scary figure but as someone so close, so safe, forever young, forever growing, someone she knew, a friend.

We learned how children are able to distill the essence of Jewish teaching and turn it into a source of inspiration. Asked "If you could have lived during any time in the Bible, when would that have been?" Davidi, age 12, answered, "At the time of the giving of the Torah at Mt. Sinai. It must have been an amazing time, just to see the Torah being given." Ronit, age 6, imagined a time even farther back: "The time of the Garden of Eden, before Adam and Eve ate the apple. I would like to have known what the world was like then."

Told of her response, a young Jewish scholar commented, "She doesn't even know how deep that answer is. She means a time before sin, when God was so close to man." But Ronit had continued, "But I like being alive now, because that's when Hashem put me here, so there must be a reason."

Collectively the children's voices gave credence to a Talmudic story explaining the very roots of the Jewish peoples' bonding with the Divine. The story is told: When the Israelites stood at Mount Sinai ready to receive the Torah, God said to them, "Bring to Me good securities to guarantee that you will observe it; then I'll give the Torah to you."

They answered, "Our ancestors will be our securities."

God answered, "I find fault with your ancestors. But bring Me good securities and I will give it [the Torah] to you."

"Our prophets will be our securities," said the Israelites.

"I find fault with your prophets," God answered.

"Our children will be our securities," offered the Israelites finally.

God answered, "Yes, for their sake, I will give you the Torah."

And so it is says in the Psalms: "Out of the mouths of babes and sucklings, you have founded strength."

As oft cited as that Psalm may have become over centuries, it stems directly from the Jewish tradition's primal connection to its children. Not only have children's expressions been ever valued in Judaism, but this source contends that its very culture was forged for their sake. Looking, as we did, at living Jewishly through the eyes of children reinforced our appreciation of this connection, for their words, whether insightful or amusing, were ultimately holy. Ours was a joyful journey of discovery, an exploration into the words, minds and souls of Jewish children. We welcome you along.

Blessed are the children who see honey in the rock.

Jonathan Mark and Ruth Seligman

I

A Chosen Child of Chosen People: What Does it Mean to Be Jewish?

What does it mean to be Jewish in the world today? Ask children and you'll find that being Jewish is defined by what Jewish people do, what they eat, how they relate to Jewish laws, rituals, beliefs, tradition and history. To some, it means simply a fact of birth; to others, it means accepting a set of responsibilities. Some children define their very Jewishness by their fulfillment of positive commandments: "Doing mitzvot is what makes me Jewish," said Jill, age 9; others, by whether they abstain from negative acts.

To some, being Jewish means being different from others in the community, or in the world-at-large. For many of these children, being different means being special. Yet for other children whose framework of life is defined by Jewish practice, everything and everyone appears to be Jewish. Take the story of Ari, age 3, who had, with his father, enjoyed watching many of the Michael Jordan games that brought the Chicago Bulls their championships. After one big win, Jordan changed out of his uniform and appeared on TV wearing a suit and tie. Ari, staring intently at Jordan's unfamiliar clothing, jumped up and said, "Look. Michael Jordan is going to shul."

Little Keith was pleased to discover the Jewishness of Arthur the Aardvark, a popular book and animated character created by author Marc Brown. Proof? Arthur celebrated Thanksgiving. After all, Thanksgiving must be a Jewish holiday; Keith goes to a

Jewish school, and they celebrate it there. And when four-year-old Helena confirmed with her parents that everyone at her day school was Jewish, she extrapolated "So if I wasn't Jewish, I wouldn't have to go to school?"

Jewish children also incorporate Jewish symbols into their life at a young age. When Alex was two, he spotted the symbol for Nike shoes on a billboard. "Look, Mommy," said Alex. "A shofar."

To some Jewish children, being Jewish means learning a different language: They go to Hebrew school, or are exposed to the Yiddish of grandparents or great-grandparents. Nevertheless, until they master these new languages, the applications can be amusing. Michali, age 4, enjoyed going to Hebrew school but something was troubling her. "Why does my teacher tell me to break my toe every day?" It was a while before her parents figured out the teacher was greeting the schoolchildren with "Boker Tov"—Hebrew for "good morning."

At the "shiva" (mourning period) for Aviva's grandmother, many people visited the house to extend condolences. As one bearded, elderly rabbi was about to leave, he asked the eight-year-old where was "the pishke"—the charity box found in most Jewish homes—so that he could make a donation in the name of the deceased. Not used to this pronunciation, rather than the more commonly heard "pushka," Aviva shyly directed the rabbi to the bathroom.

On occasion, being Jewish doesn't just mean translating from a different language, but translating a religious concept into common expression. Adam, age 4, had heard that Jews come from two original backgrounds, Ashkenaz, or European, and Sephard, Middle-Eastern or Spanish. "Mommy, are we Amish or Sephardic?" he asked, trying to pin down his family's Jewish roots. One Hebrew schoolteacher found it might be better to stick with the original language when trying to convey religious concepts. Teaching his class the famous Hanukkah song "Ma'oz Tzur," David thought his eight-year-old students might understand the English words better than the Hebrew. But he changed his mind after asking who the title "Rock of Ages" referred to. Eight-year-old Matt guessed, on behalf of all, "Elvis, maybe?"

For children in large metropolitan areas throughout the United States, being Jewish means taking advantage of hundreds of resources for Jewish education, celebration, cultural life and comradery. However, for the fraction of Jewish children in Waco,

Texas, it may mean discomfort over being "the only Jewish children in the school," as ten-year-old Martin expressed, or it may be the satisfying experience of explaining the laws and customs of Judaism in response to the frequent inquiries of friends, as it was to Martin's Hebrew school chums Natalie, Jonathan and Kalize. And in New York, "Jewish food" can easily be pizza, while in Waco it's kosher jerky.

There were as many answers to the question of what it means to be Jewish as there were children interviewed, for each had an individual insight regarding his or her heritage and how it manifested itself in his or her life.

What does it mean to be Jewish?

You celebrate Hanukkah, Succot, all the Jewish holidays. And your ancestors had a lot of hard times.

Timothy, age 8

Being Jewish means you're different from other religions and you're very close to God. He talked to our ancestors in His voice, before He talked to the other religions. God does things for us, and He helps us. We also have so many fun holidays.

Sara Noa, age 7

It means you can't have candy.

Rachel, age 4

Being Jewish means that God is going to help us, to work with us in the things we do. We believe in one God, and that we will be redeemed when the Moshiach (Messiah) comes, and then we'll live in a world that's just and peaceful.

Bruriah, age 12

It means you were chosen by God to have the Torah.

Benji, age 9

Well, I'm Jewish because I was born from my mom and she's Jewish. It also means to keep the Sabbath.

Gila, age 7

Being Jewish is a big responsibility. There are all these laws you have to follow. Sometimes there are times like Yom Kippur when you have to fast. There are some happy times, and there are some sad times, and there's always a tradition or a law in everything you do. But it pays off.

Avishai, age 10

You're not supposed to be mean when you're Jewish.

Morgan, age 10

To be Jewish means to be different. Being Christian is more publicized.

Jenna, age 11

Being Jewish makes you feel part of something. You are not alone. In the Holocaust there were people who lost entire families. But they were part of the Jewish family, so they were not alone.

Leeya, age 13

It means taking on a responsibility of keeping kosher, keeping holidays. Some people feel you don't have to keep them all, but doing them gets better the more you learn about them.

Davidi, age 12

It means you have to be nice to your parents and friends no matter what. You have rules to obey, like lighting the candles on Friday.

Anna, age 7

To be Jewish means you don't pray to idols and you don't say, "Oh, I can make a god out of clay and pray to it."

Naomi, age 7

It means you don't eat nonkosher food, you don't walk around the city naked, and you don't drop the Torah.

Ephraim, age 5

It means that we should do all of God's laws, like keep Shabbos and all the other Jewish holidays.

Ariella, age 6

You light candles at night and give money to the poor by putting money in the tzedaka box.

Rebecca, age 5

A religion is what a lot of minds have put together. You have to get people to believe in it. Someone had to start it, but it takes everyone together to get it going. I think whatever my parents do is what it means to be Jewish—to daven in the morning and celebrate holidays. You don't have to do everything if you're not religious, but people should at least celebrate the holidays because that's basically how the Jewish people started. They turned the holidays and the laws into a culture that makes the religion.

Liora, age 10

Being Jewish is really what you make of it. There are plenty of Jewish people who don't keep Shabbat (Sabbath). There are different levels of observance, but one thing that's part of being Jewish is believing there is one God.

Aliza, age 10

We're Jewish because God made us Jewish.

Peninah, age 4

I think it's important to understand the things you do as Jews. You might be raised religious and observe all the holidays without thinking about it, but it's a responsibility to understand it.

Sara, age 13

It's a responsibility. It's a practice that's been passed down through my family. Part of my family is Jewish and part is not. Some people say I get the best of both worlds, and I do, but I do like the Jewish part.

Jacob, age 12

It means to celebrate the holidays and be nice and good to people.

Talia, age 7

You have to listen to the Ten Commandments, do mitzvahs, pray and celebrate the holidays and I forget what else.

Bobbie, age 6

To be Jewish means to talk softly, and wear yarmulkes, tzitzit, and also not to get hurt.

Sam, age 5

It means to worry about finding your kipah (yarmulke).

Etan, age 8

We're the only ones with the Ten Commandments.

Alisha, age 10

It means not to bow to statues.

Mutti, age 8

It means to celebrate the Jewish holidays, the traditions and the customs that make us Jewish.

Josh, age 11

What do Jewish people do?

They keep the Ten Commandments and read the Torah every Saturday.

Benji, age 9

Follow the Torah.

Allie, age 12

Plenty of other religions believe there is just one God, but what I do, like going to synagogue, following certain restrictions on Shabbat and other days, praying every day—that makes me Jewish.

Aliza, age 10

Jews do stuff like every normal person and they have holidays like other religions, but they don't eat all the same foods. They also do lots of fun stuff.

Sara, age 7

We do a lot of Hebrew, we do a lot of prayer and we don't speak bad.

Lauren, age 7

Jews are basically good people. If they can avoid fighting they will. When you're in first or second grade, we learn things we're supposed to do, like what we're supposed to eat, and what we're not supposed to.

Liora, age 10

They eat, go to sleep, have jobs, and go swimming in the summer.

Simeon, age 11

They're like everyone else. They just celebrate different holidays.

Anne, age 7

Some Jews have different customs, so it's not like all Jews do the same thing. But praying is one thing that all Jews do.

Avishai, age 10

Jewish people celebrate a lot of holidays.

Rebecca, age 8

Jewish people bow to the real God.

Mutti, age 8

They're polite when they go to the bathroom.

Etan, age 8

Jewish people have a lot of holidays because the holidays are about what happened in the past and they have to remember that.

Ian, age 9

They go to synagogue and every Friday they celebrate Shabbat.

Anna, age 7

Jewish people pray to God so they can get more mitzvahs.

Chai, age 6

What do Jewish people believe?

Jewish people believe that God is real and He created the world and the universe.

Benji, age 9

Jewish people believe in the Torah. Other people believe in their atmosphere, in what's around them.

Allie, age 12

Jewish people believe in God and Moses.

Timothy, age 8

Jewish people think the world is a good place, and not a place for slavery.

Samantha, age 7

Jewish people believe in only one God, and they have all these traditions.

Avishai, age 10

They believe in Adam and Eve, Abraham and Sarah.

Martin, age 10

Jewish people believe that there's reasons for all the punishments we get.

Dora, age 9

They believe in one God, not two.

Anna, age 7

Jewish people believe that one day a man or woman named Moshiach (Messiah) will come and that one day everyone will come back, not in a scary way, but how they were before they were dead, but not bad people, and that everyone will be happy and live in Jerusalem.

Rivka, age 6

They believe in God. They believe in the Torah; they believe all the stories in the Bible and they do *not* believe you should pray to an idol.

Sara, age 6

They believe in God and in celebrating the Shabbat.

Danit, age 8

They believe in Moses.

Cort, age 8

Jewish people do not believe in statues. They only believe in one God.

Ariella, age 6

2

In Touch with God

Awesome, invisible, all powerful, God is nevertheless anything but inaccessible to Jewish children. Children told us how God extends greetings when they come into synagogue, and how He accompanies them home. He's there when their team plays basketball and, they hope, when the teacher gives a test. To some children, God is a She, to others a bit of both, with the trees, sky and the songs of birds thrown in. Children learn early that one of the Ten Commandments warns against creating an image of God, but that doesn't mean they don't sense His presence everywhere.

Dari, for example, goes often with her father to pray at the ancient Western Wall in Jerusalem, because Abba (Hebrew for father) feels closest to God there. When the pair comes home and Dari eats her sandwich, Abba reminds her to say the blessing thanking God. Dari does so and then waves her hand in the direction of the Wall. "Okay, God. You can go home now," she says.

Rachel's house, too, apparently received a visit from God. The four-year-old paid increasing attention to her pregnant mother's swelling stomach. "I know there's a baby in there, and I know how it got there," said Rachel. "God put it there."

Eight-year-old Micah was consumed with learning script writing. Thus, when his mother tucked him into bed on Rosh Hashanah and reminded him that God was writing his fate for the coming year, Micah asked the cosmic question so important to a third grader: "Is God writing in cursive or printing?"

Shumi was conscious of God's presence in her home one Friday evening. Watching her daughter grow impatient waiting for her father to come home, Mom suggested she cut out one of the puzzles in the *Ladybug* magazine the four-year-old finally became interested in. "Oh no. That would be mean to God," came the answer. And two-year-old Becca was known for dallying at every task, but one morning in particular she seemed to be taking extra time in the bathroom. When Dad walked in to see what was the delay, he found her waving her arm in the air, toothbrush in hand. "I'm busy. I'm brushing God's teeth."

Dari, Micah, Shumi, Rachel and Becca's familiarity and sense of comfort with God's presence was typical of the feelings of the children we spoke with. So, too, was Elie and Nathaniel's sense of God being everywhere. The four-year-old twins engaged in an impassioned discussion of God one night before their bedtime ritual of reciting the Sh'ma. One asked, "Is God up in the sky?" "Yes," Dad answered. "Is God in us?" they asked in unison. "Yes," came the answer again. Finally, after more discussion back and forth, one twin asked, "Is God in the grass? Because if He is, if a cow eats grass, would he be eating God?"

Tsvi, at age 3, became concerned about preserving God's eternal transcendence during a discussion about life and death. He already knew that there's a little bit of God inside everyone. Thus, while considering the death of his grandfather for whom he was named, Tsvi concluded: "God decides when people will die, and I will die, too. The same God who made me will decide when I will die. But before I die the little bit of God that's inside me will rush out."

It was God's omnipotence that impressed four-year-old Micha. He had learned through a puppet show in school that God had "created the animals, the plants, and everything." After all, Micha explained excitedly, this was "God of the University." Yael was not only impressed by God's work. She found in it a role model. Yael knows that "babies come from their mommy's tummy, dad puts them there, and they are just a little seed and then grow into babies." The four-year-old only wanted to know how God puts people into the little seed. Mom couldn't answer, because, she said, "Only God knows how He does it." Yael thought for a few seconds, and then said, "Mommy, one day I want to be God."

Who is God? To children, God is their intimate ally.

Who is God?

Nobody is as smart as God. He made everything, so He knows how everything works. He even made movie theaters.

Elana, age 4

I think he looks like a man that's very old, but he doesn't have a beard. He also looks really young, like thirty-seven years old, but He's probably seven trillion years old. God's right here but I can't see Him.

Cort, age 8

God is the person Who created us, our home and our food and the creatures and everything. He is the king of angels Who can create anything you want. That's an easy one.

Rebecca, age 5

God created the world. Before that everything was in a mess. But first God said, "Let there be light," because He had to have light to clean up the mess.

Avital, age 4

God must be a woman because we are all God's children and only women can have children.

Katie, age 4

He looks like everything because He is everything.

Lauren, age 7

I think God is a burning bush.

Morgan, age 8

The sun.

Leah, age 6

The world is God's dollhouse and we're His dolls. He presses buttons and makes us talk and walk.

Elana, age 5

God is the creator of the world and the universe and me. He provides food, water and everything else we need.

Benji, age 9

He's a spirit that's the brother of Gayus, the queen of the forest.

Cort, age 8

God is everywhere.

Marla, age 8

God could be anywhere. He might be in the sky, He might be in the ocean. He could be in somebody's house.

Richard, age 5

He's really big. He's even in outer space.

David, age 5

God made us. He also made the flowers, the plants and bananas.

Peninah, age 4

He's not a man. He's not a woman. He's our God. He created us and He created the universe, so He's king of the universe.

Jesse, age 7

God is in the sky and nobody can see Him because He is every-where. He's also in the ground.

Sam, age 5

Somebody up there.

Ethan, age 4

I think he's a swarm of colors that creates life on this planet.

Martin, age 10

God is a beautiful lady in a beautiful white dress. She sits in heaven with Her dress spread all around Her. It covers the earth and protects us.

Tracy, age 5

God is a mighty powerful spirit.

Zoe, age 6

God is an invisible being Who Jewish people love and pray to.

Moriah, age 6

It's the air, the spirit, and the energy floating around.

Anna, age 7

He's all around the place. He listens.

Madeline, age 5

The ceiling and the wall and the floor.

Rachel, age 4

God is the ruler of the world and He was always there.

Noah, age 9

God lives in the world and in the Temple, which is His house. When the blue light is on over the Ark where the Torahs are, that means He's home.

Richard, age 4

What does God do?

God makes the world round. If it gets straight He gets really, really mad.

Grace, age 4

God makes people be alive. Since He created the world, He makes sure it keeps going by making more seeds and more stores. He makes sure no one person could be in a pickle, like when you can't make up your mind.

Moriah, age 6

God sits around and helps people.

Tamar, age 6

Nowadays, God helps the plants grow.

Gila, age 7

God is the person who watches out for you and protects you.

Esther, age 6

God watches people and watches over the world. He made the grass and the sky.

Max, age 5

He helps people and does things for people in every way He can.

Allie, age 12

God stays in heaven and does stuff, like talks to the people that are dead.

Michael, age 6

He makes good things happen. He creates rain.

Cort, age 8

God watches people and helps them. And if someone is bad, He pops something into their body to make them stop being bad.

Nechama, age 7

When we pray, He answers our prayers either yes or no.

Brian, age 9

He creates people. He creates more land. He watches over everyone.

Grace, age 7

He tells us to daven when it's Shabbos.

Rachel, age 4

He makes the people that kill His trees and His animals suffer, because on "National Geographic" once—I don't know whether this was fake or not—but they showed this man cutting off a tree and the tree didn't land on him but somehow he was holding it and he died. He also makes spiders and praying mantises to kill other bugs that try to kill life.

Martin, age 10

God is relaxing on the beach.

Sherry, age 8

He gives us life. He gives us food.

Lauren, age 7

God makes buildings, houses and cities.

Rachel, age 5

God makes new babies and He protects people when there's a war or something.

Anna, age 7

He tries to fix people's lives. I don't know what else He does, because I'm not Him.

David, age 9

He spends time saving people from being slaves.

Brendan, age 7

God made buildings and people, fruits and vegetables, onions and tomatoes, cucumbers and wheat.

Hila, age 4

He didn't make buildings. He made trees and people use them to make buildings.

Lena, age 4

What does God do for you?

When my parents were at their wedding, God was my baby-sitter.

Shira, age 4

God makes you Jewish.

Ephraim, age 5

God gives us food, listens to us pray and gave us the Torah.

Josh, age 7

God gave me talents.

Timothy, age 8

If something really bad happens, you can ask God to make it not happen. God helps you with your thinking if you don't want to think.

Brendan, age 7

God is watching us every day.

Grace, age 4

He keeps all my pets alive, except for my hamster. Well, He tried. He gives me friends so I'm not bored after school.

Morgan, age 8

You could ask Him to get you a drink if there was no more water around anywhere.

Lena, age 4

He gives food. He would also tell me to go to school.

Rachel, age 4

He takes care of us.

Martin, age 10

God should be the first one in your life, because He's been with you even when you were in your mother's stomach.

Samantha, age 9

When we feel alone we can always go to God.

Sara, age 13

I know God will always help me if I do good things. The Temple was destroyed because all the Jews weren't doing good things, so He let the other side win.

Nichole, age 9

God gives me the toys I want, a good family, a good school, a good mother and good friends.

Benji, age 9

He answers my wishes.

Allie, age 12

He takes care of me. He's basically like my parents, but He's one person. I mean, my parents take care of me, but God takes care of them, and without God I wouldn't have parents.

Avishai, age 10

If anyone is in the desert, God gives them food to survive.

Brendan, age 7

Ever since He created the world, God has been making it better, and saving it. Our house burnt down, but He saved our family.

Liora, age 10

God makes miracles. He let me be born.

Nina, age 7

What are you thankful to God for?

My family, good friends, good food.

Benji, age 9

I'm thankful that I'm here.

Nina, age 7

For bringing me here.

Timothy, age 8

I am thankful that I have two parents who love me very much, a wonderful family, a wonderful school, wonderful camp and wonderful friends.

Allie, age 12

I thank God for waking me up. Every day when I wake up, it's like God is giving my soul a new chance to be good.

Sara Noa, age 7

For all the food.

Rachel, age 4

For my family, my friends Adam and Emmy, and 1995, the year I was born.

Nicholas, age 3

I thank God for making pumpkins. They're beautiful, they're orange and you can eat every part of them, even the seeds.

Joel, age 5

I'm thankful to God that my parents adopted me.

Shawn, age 9

For a great Mommy and Daddy.

Gabriella, age 4

I thank God for all the wonderful things He did.

Benny, age 5

I'm thankful for just everything that is happening in my life.

Liora, age 10

I thank God for what we have, and I don't need another thing.

Anna, age 7

Having friends.

Michelle, age 9

I'm thankful for great parents.

Rachel, age 5

I'm thankful for my whole family. They're really special. I just love them.

Richard, age 4

I thank God for a great sister.

Lauren, age 4

For giving me everything I have.

Gila, age 7

I'm thankful for trees because they give us oxygen.

Miriam, age 7

I'm thankful that I was born because I get to see exciting things go on.

Samantha, age 7

I'm thankful to God for giving us a baby.

Grace, age 4

I thank him for my family, and all the other people in the family, like my cousins, aunts, uncles, grandmothers and grandfathers. I thank him that the Moshiach will come soon so I can see my grandfathers.

Rebecca, age 6

I thank God for giving us birds.

Micky, age 6

I thank God for letting people talk.

Emily, age 7

I thank God for making all the trees and for making us all have a good life.

Brendan, age 7

For making me a beautiful family.

Esther, age 6

I'm thankful for Him giving me parents and I'm thankful for a house and all my food and my clothes.

Esther, age 9

I'm thankful to God for making me, for giving me a nice happy and healthy life and for having a very big family.

Noah, age 9

We learn that people are created "in the image of God." What do you think that means?

He made us kind of like Him, like we all have the same feelings.

Allana, age 6

He made us like Him, because maybe He knows we'll think like him.

Josh, age 11

It's not exactly how they look, but how they are. God is like a nice guy. He doesn't steal or anything, and He wants us to be nice, too.

Daisy, age 9

We were all created by God, and we have feelings like Him. I think when someone is born on a day when God is unhappy, those people are unhappy for the rest of their lives.

Harry, age 9

God made a couple of mistakes, like sometimes people are too greedy. Or in the story of Noah and the Ark, God made all these people who didn't treat each other nicely, so He had to start over and fill the world with good people. Since we're created in God's image, we learn we can make mistakes and not everything will be totally terrific.

Dara, age 9

It means we know a lot of things like God, and we're good like God.

Tal, age 6

God has many images, so since He has tons of images, He created each one of us in different images to represent different parts of Him.

Avishai, age 10

It means we're both alive.

Yona, age 6

It means we were created with a little bit of God inside of us. An image is just a little piece of a picture, so that little bit that is God's image could be our conscience.

Aliza, age 10

3

The Bible: Great Tales and Superheroes

No book a child can read is more filled with mystery, excitement, adventure and heroic deeds than the Bible. The world comes into being from nothing and is formed in six days, complete with sun, stars, moon, grass, seas and animals of every kind. A snake speaks and changes the destiny of humankind forever. Noah builds an ark and fills it with two of every animal and floats along safely with this menagerie through a forty-day flood. Abraham smashes his father's idols and declares there is one God. Sarah bears a son deep in her old age. Jacob wrestles with an angel. Joseph mystically interprets dreams and gains a powerful appointment in Pharaoh's court as his reward. The Jews become slaves in Egypt, but baby Moses is rescued from a basket bobbing along the Nile. God speaks to Moses from inside a burning bush and sends fearsome plagues to free His Jewish people. They flee into a surging sea that splits into dry land, and the people become a nation amidst the fire and thunder of Mount Sinai, where the Ten Commandments are forged.

All this is the Torah. Then come the tales of prophets and kings: Jonah, who was swallowed by a great fish; David, who slew the mighty Goliath; Solomon the wise. And finally come the books of heroism and noble deeds: Queen Esther saves the Jews of ancient Persia; the Maccabees triumph over tyranny. Could any literary heritage be more dramatic?

For Jewish children, stories from the weekly Torah portion, or the later biblical narratives the children themselves act out in Hanukkah and Purim plays, inform the imagination and paint the backdrop of Jewish identity. Superheroes abound in their very own culture and are a source of inspiration. Take Marti, for instance, whose mother asked casually if her daughter bows to her karate teacher, a common practice in martial arts classes. "No!" came the reply. "I would only bow to God!" It was only days after the celebration of Purim, in which the story of Mordechai's refusal to bow to the tyrant Haman is elaborately recalled. Sam, age 5, even found in the Bible a way to express his displeasure to his mother over every child's perennial perception of being treated less fairly than a sister or brother. "Ima," he told his mom. "You're like Jacob, who loved Joseph more."

For some children, those superheroes have a personal connection, for the children bear their names. Asked who freed the Jews from slavery in Egypt, three-year-old Moshe's proud answer was, "I did." Four-year-old Rebecca decided to become a veterinarian because the biblical Rebecca demonstrated the importance of caring for animals by fetching water for thirsty camels.

Do the children have a favorite Bible story? Is there a character they would like to have met? Their answers say indeed they do.

Can you tell any stories from the Bible?

In the story of Jonah, Jonah was very greedy. There were too many people on the boat and God told Jonah to jump in the water because then the people would be saved.

Chad, age 12

At the end of the Passover story, the water opened up for the Jewish people.

Shlomiya, age 4

One of my favorite stories from the Bible is about Rebecca at the well. She gave Eliezer water for himself and for his camels. This story is yummy.

Allie, age 12

Noah heard God telling him he needed to build an ark because there was going to be a flood and he needed to bring two of every animal into the ark. The people laughed at him, but he was the one who survived.

Mikka, age 10

In the story of Noah, God sent the flood and He told Noah to build an ark to save himself because Noah was a peaceful person. God made a mistake with everyone else but Noah.

Martin, age 10

In the story of Moses they were gonna kill all the baby boys so his mom made a basket and floated him away, and he ended up with the Pharoah's daughter, so when he grew up he finally found out he was a Jew, so he asked Pharoah and Pharoah said no, and they were making bread and the bread didn't have time to rise so that's how they got matzah for Passover, and then he led the Jews and he opened the water and patched it shut. It doesn't say this in any movie or anything but he had to get two people to bury him under the sand before they crossed the Jordan River because Moses banged the rock instead of tapped it, so God told him to stay. He didn't have to, but he listened to God's command. No one knows where he was buried because he didn't want anyone to know and he chose those two people to bury him because they were never going to come back after they crossed the Jordan River.

Arielle, age 9

In the exodus from Egypt, the Pharoah had all these Jewish people for slaves, and somebody or something told Moses he must go and save these people and he tried all these plagues, and the Pharoah kept changing his mind and finally he let them go.

Natalie, age 11

In the story of Passover, we celebrate the Ten Commandments or plagues, which Moses told King Pharoah about, and he didn't listen. The Pharoah didn't listen to the tenth plague the night that the Jews listened to Moses and put sheep's blood all over their door so they could protect their child. Except the Pharoah and all the Egyptians didn't know what they were doing that for, so they didn't listen, and that night the Ten Commandments struck and this kind of fog came and killed every Egyptian child except in houses that had sheep blood over it.

Morgan, age 8

Esther saved her people from being destroyed because she had a key person put away from the king. I think it was King Roger. Here's the story. Esther and the king fell in love, got married and that man Haman found out she was Jewish. He was one of the kings and he said he would like to kill all the Jews because they were nasty people and the king said, "Yes. OK." And then David—I think it was—told his sister, Queen Esther, what would happen. And he told her, "You have to tell the king who you really are," and she told the king she was really a Jew, and "If you kill Haman you're going to kill me." So instead of Esther being killed, Haman was sent far, far away.

Martin, age 10

In Jonah and the whale, Jonah had a mission to God to do something in this city. I don't know the city's name. But he was on a ship and it started raining because of him and the ship was about to sink and then Jonah told the guys on the ship to throw him out to sea and a whale ate him, but he stayed alive— I don't know how—but then the whale had stomach indigestion. I don't know what happened but he got puked out into the sea, and he did his task in whatever city it was and he was a better person.

Jonathan, age 11

In the story of Passover, Moses led the Jews out of Egypt to a new place, where it would be safe, and he struck the river in half so the Israelites could cross the ocean and when all the Israelites were gone and the Pharoah and his warriors were running across he struck the river in half and he let the waters fall on them and he let them drown.

Cort, age 8

In the story of Noah, everybody in the whole world was being bad. They weren't following any rules or anything. So God asked Noah—he was like the only good person in his family—to put two of every animal in his ark and God made it rain for forty days and forty nights and Noah sent out a bird and it left and it didn't come back and then he sent out a dove and the dove came back with an olive branch and then there was a rainbow and everything dried up and the rainbow was a promise from God that He wouldn't do that again.

Halyn, age 12

In the story of Hanukkah, the Jews were in the desert, and the Jews needed oil and the miracle was that the oil lasted for eight days.

Daniel, age 12

In the story of Passover, Hashem gave Moses all these things to do so that the Egyptians would believe him. Hashem gave him three miracles—when you tap your staff, it will turn into a snake. If you tap water with your staff, it turns to blood. If you tap the staff, a whole bunch of frogs will come. So he goes and does the first miracle. Then the children were good with magic. They said magic words and alligator-suited people came. Moses did the ten plagues. Finally, after the tenth plague, Pharaoh let them leave. Pharaoh started to follow. The Red Sea split and the Jews ran across. When the Egyptians went into the water, it closed over them and they drowned.

Benji, age 9

Esther was a Jew and there was this prince and he wanted to marry her so she would be queen. And over in the other side of the city, Haman was threatening to kill the Jews, and she hadn't really heard of it until this certain time. She was queen and she had not told her husband and the reason why she didn't tell was because she thought he was just going to kick her out and order her to be killed like all the rest of the Jews but one day she told and he did not get mad and she wanted to save her people and so Haman had this little thing that hangs people and she comes out and saves the Jews and then they found out that Haman did all of this, so they hung him on the thing he was supposed to hang the Jews with.

Samantha, age 9

This is about the Maccabees. It all started when the Jews—they were just praying in the Temple and the Philistines did not like the way they prayed. They wanted the Jews to follow their own ways. So they just came and banged down the Temple. So the Jews made up this name the Maccabees, which means hammer, and they had this all-day battle. The Philistines outnumbered the Maccabees but the Maccabees still won. Then they went to the Temple to find oil to last one day, that's all they needed, but a miracle happened that the oil lasted for eight days.

Ricky, age 9

In the story of Judah and the Maccabees, Judah was the one who got fed up about having to pray on statues that weren't even real and so he told his fellow Maccabees that if they had enough people they could fight and probably win with God on their side. They fought and Judah died during the war and three of his four sons died and the youngest kept on fighting for the right of freedom.

Martin, age 10

Do you have a favorite story or character from the Bible? Is there a time during biblical days when you would like to have been alive?

Moses is one of my favorites. He inspires me because of the way he worked for the people. He showed that he cared.

Bruria, age 12

Moses because he's a leader, and Abraham because he was the first one who believed in God.

Benji, age 9

Abraham is one of the best. He listened to God. He was the first one who listened to God.

David, age 5

Adam. Because that's my name, and also, he was the first guy.

Adam, age 9

God.

Morgan, age 8

I would like to have lived in the time of Gan Eden (the Garden of Eden) so I could see what it was like there before Adam and Eve ate the apple. But I want to be here now because this is where God put me, so there must be a reason.

Ronit, age 6

I liked Eve, because she was the first woman.

Mabrie, age 10

Rachel. She was the nicest person in the Torah. Everybody else did something mean, but not Rachel. Leah was the nicest, too.

Richard, age 5

Esther, because she does good deeds.

Ariella, age 6

I would like to have been there at the time of the giving of the Torah at Mt. Sinai. It must have been an amazing time, just to see the Torah. My favorite person in the Bible might be David. He's an unexpected kind of guy. He's there in this field working, and then he's supposed to be king. My favorite person could have been Goliath. He was tall enough to be a center in basketball.

Davidi, age 12

Moshe, because I think the story about him in the Bible is very exciting. He's one of the most exciting people in the Torah. He was a leader in Israel.

Ronit, age 6

I like Abraham, Isaac, Jacob and Moses because they all did good things and they liked to pray.

Meir, age 4

Moses. During his life he had some really neat stuff happen to him, like the burning bush, leading the people out of Egypt and how that stick made the waters split in half. I think it's just neat. The plagues and all that stuff.

Samantha, age 9

Moses and Jonathan, David's friend. Because he has my name and because I heard lots of good things about him. And Moses was really special.

Jonathan, age 11

I like the Maccabees because I like adventure stories. I did not like Eve because she the took fruit from the snake.

Ben, age 12

I would like to have lived in the time of Rahel to meet her. I like her. She was competitive with her sister, Leah, and Jacob's other wives. She must have been something because Jacob waited for her for fourteen years. I would also like to have known Sarah and Rivka. They each had one good son and one bad. I would like to learn how to live with that. I guess my top five from the Bible would be Esther, Sarah, Rivka, Rahel, Miriam, Leah, Rahav and Naomi. That's more than five.

Liora, age 10

I don't know if he's that big of a character, but I like Jacob in Jacob and Esau, because he was a twin and I'm a twin, and he was the younger one, and I'm the younger one. I just like him because he's cool.

Daniel, age 11

Moses was very kind and he obeyed God. Also Noah. While he was building the ark, some people made fun of him but he didn't stop because of their opinions. He kept on going because that is what God told him to do.

Mikkah, age 10

Moses, because he was always patient. Except for one time when he wasn't patient because he hit the rock or something. Anyway, that's what my mom has to work on. I also like the Maccabees because they fought back.

Gila, age 7

Rebecca, because I'm named after her, and she married Isaac. And Moses had a speech impediment, so I think that was cool that Aaron spoke for him.

Rebecca, age 12

I like the bad guys like Pharoah and Haman. Without the bad guys, the stories wouldn't be too interesting.

Ricky, age 9

Queen Esther was really brave to tell Ahasveros what Haman wanted to do to the Jews. I think she saved the Jews from that position.

Arielle, age 9

I'm inspired by Cain and Abel because I have a little sister and we fight all the time and that's sort of a shame. I learn not to fight with my sibling.

Sophia, age 9

I didn't like Joseph because he was his father's favorite.

Mabrie, age 11

I like God, because He made us, and if He didn't make us I wouldn't be here, and I wouldn't have Elsie for a friend, and Ashley for a friend, and Alicia for a friend and I wouldn't be so smart and I wouldn't be able to pass my '98 assessment and go to the mall. I hated Pharoah because he always hurt the Jews and punished them and slapped them with a stick.

Morgan, age 8

I like Jacob. He was pretty clever. He had a dream that he was fighting an angel. God was really testing if Jacob could fight and he did pretty good.

Anna, age 7

I like the Joseph's ark story. Or somebody's ark. I don't like Hangman (Haman).

Chance, age 10

My favorite Bible heroine is Rachel, because she didn't want to embarrass her sister. I thought she was nice.

Yael, age 9

I like the story of Adam and Eve. It teaches us that you really can*not* do what you are told not to do.

Jerry, age 8

I like Moses and I hate the Pharaoh. If it wasn't for Moses, we'd still be slaves in Egypt. Moses was the only one God trusted to save the Jews. Moses was the chosen one. Pharaoh is the one who said Jews aren't made to be free.

Martin, age 10

I like Samson because he was a great hero. He was brave and he inspires me to be brave.

Dana, age 11

I like Esther because she was pretty.

Ariella, age 7

I like Mordechai. He wouldn't let people boss him around.

Eliot, age 4

Judah Maccabee. He was a warrior. He was one of the knights of Israel.

Cort, age 8

Batya, Pharaoh's daughter, and Moses. I like Batya because if she hadn't saved Moses from being killed by Pharaoh, Moses wouldn't have been able to save the Jews. So if Batya wasn't born, the Jews would still be slaves in Egypt and they wouldn't live in America, or get to go to fun places like Sportstime USA.

Becky, age 6

My favorite Jewish personality is Rachel, Rabbi Akiva's wife. She left her father for some nobody who she hoped would be great in Torah. If it wasn't for her, we wouldn't have any Rabbi Akiva.

Kaley, age 10

I like Samuel. He got David and Solomon to be kings. That shows he's sort of an organizer. He was good at getting things together.

Evan, age 9

I like Moses because he led the Jews to freedom. Also, we learn from Moses not to scream, because he screamed at the rock when he was trying to get water and then God wouldn't let him go into Israel.

Ariella, age 6

I like Noah, from Noah and the Ark. Even though the people didn't believe him he still believed in God. I'm not sure if that could really happen but it inspires you to never give up what you believe.

Jack, age 11

I also like Judah Maccabee. He led the Maccabees in the fight for freedom against the Romans. And David. All I know was that he was a star and he slayed Goliath.

Martin, age 10

4

The Torah, the Ten Commandments and Jewish Law

Rachel, age 7, and her brother, Ari, age 4, ran into the living room, lay down on opposite sides of the room and rolled toward each other yelling, "Look! We're a Torah scroll!"

The centerpiece of Jewish observance is the Torah—the five Books of Moses describing the early history of Judaism and its founders, of the Jewish people's enslavement and exodus from Egypt, and their forty years of wandering in the desert while God and Moses worked to forge them into a nation by binding them to Jewish law before their entry into the Promised Land.

Contained within the Torah are the Ten Commandments, which are repeated within the Torah narrative. The children quickly learn at least one of these by heart: Honor thy mother and father. A convenient assist to establishing familial respect, it sets these relationships into a comforting context of doing the right thing not only within the family but within the sight of God. The commandments are also the core of all the laws of Jewish observance—all 613 of them. These are delineated in, or extrapolated from, various Torah portions. A portion of the Torah is read in the synagogue each week, with the entire Torah completed annually, beginning on the holiday of Simchat Torah in the autumn and concluded when the next Simchat Torah rolls around a year later.

To chant the Torah portion aloud in the synagogue is most

often what constitutes the right of passage for boys at their Bar Mitzvah—the time when they accept the mantle of religious majority at age thirteen. Within the last few decades, chanting the Torah portion, or offering commentary in a "d'var Torah" sermonette, has also increasingly become a right of passage for girls becoming Bat Mitzvah at age twelve.

So central is the Torah to Jewish observance and ritual that children know about it from a very young age. Soft plush Torahs are a gift to babies at birth and to toddlers on the holiday of Simchat Torah. Making a "Torah scroll" is a perennial art project for Sunday schools and Jewish craft days at Jewish centers. Thus, when Rachel and Ari acted out the part of a Torah scroll being rolled and unrolled in the synagogue, their mom was amused—but not surprised.

And when Noah, age 4, encountered a small moral problem, he and his parents engaged in a form of traditional scholarship to parse out the biblical source of his dilemma: Noah had received many picture books telling the story of Noah and the Ark. His parents read him the story dozens of times, always connecting the idea that he was named after the Noah in the Bible. One day, he came home from a store with candy that he had not paid for. His parents asked why he'd taken it, and Noah responded, "God told me to take it."

His parents were stumped. Dared they tell him God did not talk to little Noah when they had told him so many times how God commanded the original Noah to build the ark? Finally, they told their son, even if God told him to take the candy, Noah must not have heard the part about paying for it, since God would never allow him to steal.

What does it say in the Torah, and what do we learn from it? What, exactly, are the Ten Commandments, and how do we fulfill Jewish law? The children offered the following thoughts.

What is the Torah? What's in it and what do we learn from it?

The rules.

Avital, age 6

It's something God gave to the Jewish people because they
didn't ask what was inside it.

Gila, age 7

The Torah is a very long scroll that has stories and things about
the Jewish people and about important Jewish people in the
past. It also has prayers.

Rickie, age 6

The Torah is a special, special book. The Bible is in it and that
has stories of what happened a long time ago. God gave it to us
and we learn stories, we learn Jewish stuff and we learn morals.

Geri, age 7

The Torah tells us no fighting, no teasing, we have to pray. It
also tells us everybody's picture is pretty.

Rivka, age 4

The Torah is important because you have to remember what
went on in our past. It tells us what happened with our ancestors and it's our history. It teaches you that you should always
remember what happened to you in all situations. It's a tradition
to read from it every week, to keep it alive and remember it,
because people have been reading it for so long. It's also fun to
read because of all the stories.

Jacob, age 12

The Torah is how Jews identify themselves. If you're a
Christian, you have Christian laws. If you're a Muslim, you
have something else. But the Torah is what makes you a
Jewish person.

Liora, age 10

The Torah has God's name and the story of Noah and the Ark.
They got out of the flood, and God sent a rainbow.

Ayelet, age 4

The Torah tells us to do mitzvahs, like say a blessing on food.

Ali, age 4

It tells about all the people you can't remember, and it gives you Abraham's family tree.

Joe, age 10

The Torah is there for us to learn morals. Like the story of Miriam tells us not to gossip.

Alex, age 11

The Torah teaches us to do good things and know about how things were back then and how we should appreciate the things we have now.

Tali, age 7

What are the Ten Commandments?

Aren't there fifteen?

Allen, age 9

Don't commit adultery. But I don't know what that means.

Gila, age 7

Don't do bad things. Don't say bad things, don't be afraid, recycle, do what's always right, be peaceful and never do something that you don't want to do just because someone tells you to.

Alex, age 10

The Ten Commandments are two pieces of whatever they used for paper in those days. God tells us what He wants us to do in them, like respect your parents, go to synagogue, don't blame someone like if you broke a picture frame and your father or mother says, "Who did this," you shouldn't say your cousin did it.

Yona, age 6

There are actually not ten commandments. There are one hundred sixty thousand.

Jonathan, age 11

They're laws for the Jewish people. It's like our rules on what we should do and what we should not do, except some people don't listen to them.

Arielle, age 9

There's some stuff in them I think you should obey, not just blow them off. You don't have to follow all of them, but sometimes I think that would be the mature thing to do.

Lacey, age 12

Don't steal, don't be jealous, obey your mother and father—that's the fifth. Be kind and welcome somebody. Like if somebody comes to your house you shouldn't be mean to them.

Richard, age 5

The Ten Commandments are plagues to the Egyptians.

Martin, age 10

They're rules we have to obey—everybody in the whole world has to.

Mabrie, age 11

Be nice to your neighbor. Don't say I hate you. I mean, even though that's not one of the commandments, that's just plum rude. You don't have to follow them. It's not like you have to do this or you'll get in big trouble. Some of the commandments you do because you should just try to be good, so they're important to know.

Samantha, age 9

The Ten Commandments are be nice to your father, never forget about God and obey all the rules.

Anna, age 7

Be loyal to God.

Morgan, age 8

They're like a Jewish golden rule. Like, thou shalt not take God's name in covet.

Ricky, age 9

One is not to commit adultery. That's when a man or woman
has someone else in their life, like on Ricky Lake or Jerry
Springer.

Brian, age 9

Everybody goes by the Ten Commandments—Christians and Jews.

Max, age 12

I am your God; you may not have any visions of Me and you
may not have any other gods; honor your mother and father;
don't kill; don't kidnap; don't be a false witness; don't be jealous.

Avishai, age 10

Don't play with matches.

Zachary, age 4

They're Jewish rules we follow. We try very hard to do them but
sometimes we can't follow all of them.

Mikkah, age 10

God gave us the Ten Commandments when we got out of
Egypt because the people probably felt free to do anything after
being slaves for so long, and maybe they would forget God, so
He told them, "Honor thy God." That's one of the most
important ones. Also, don't be jealous.

Josh, age 11

There's don't commit adultery. That's what President Clinton did.

Ben, age 12

Obey your parents and be kind to your neighbors.

Terry, age 10

Don't hit somebody.

Lizzie, age 4

They say not to write God's name, but I think you can, because
when you throw away the paper you write it on, it goes into the
ground and then you can recycle it.

Rebecca, age 11

It says pizza is kosher, and challah is kosher.

Jack, age 4

You should not covet, like want something that someone else has.

Rebecca, age 12

I think they all start with thou.

Daniel, age 12

We had been slaves in Egypt and there was always someone telling us what to do. Maybe He felt that when we were free, we wouldn't follow any rules anymore. We already knew not to murder or steal, but He had to tell us the rest of the rules.

Adam, age 11

Honor your parents because we didn't have to be born and we should thank them by honoring them.

Allie, age 12

You shall not sleep with another mate.

Halyn, age 12

Honor your parents. We honor our parents because without them we wouldn't be here. They deserve a lot of respect. There's also: Do not worship anyone or anything but God. Don't use God's name in vain. That's all I can think of.

Benji, age 9

Don't dishonor your father, or God will punish you. Don't smoke.

Timothy, age 8

Don't lie. Be kind to others. Love your family. No stealing.

Grace, age 7

To be good.

Peninah, age 4

Don't push. Don't hit. That's all I know.

Benny, age 5

You shouldn't fight. No pushing. No kicking people out of their job.

Max, age 5

There's five senses. No killing policemen.

Maddie, age 5

5

The Jewish Calendar, Part I: Remember the Sabbath to Keep It Holy

Yehudit awoke early one Saturday morning in Jerusalem. She ran to her mother and grabbed her by the hand. "Mommy, look at that sky. See the little white clouds and the pretty colors? Mommy, that's a Shabbat sky."

The Jewish calendar is graced each week by a special time—a day that serves as an oasis from the rushing hustle of every day life. The seventh day, the Sabbath day, was established by God in the Ten Commandments as a day of rest, to commemorate the resting God indulged in upon completing the awesome task of creating the world. Certainly, there are weeks in the lives of all modern families today that seem awesomely exhausting, even awesomely creative, and the opportunity to sit back for even a moment's reflection is welcomed by many.

In some Jewish families, Sabbath is marked by the ritual of candle lighting, synagogue attendance, festive meals and study. Even where observance of the laws is less stringent, the Sabbath meal may be the only one during the week a family manages to share together, touching the household atmosphere with holiness. Carrie, age 2, already knows that feeling. She has two lawyers for parents and a new baby brother. So busy is Mom these days that she rarely sets the table before a meal. When she does, only one thing is possible in Carrie's mind. "It's Shabbos?" Carrie asks.

Sabbath may simply mean a sense of family time, a day to visit grandparents or take a walk in the park. However it is marked, Shabbat, Shabbos, the Sabbath has served to sustain both Jewish life and the lives of Jews for millennia. Even the youngest understand what Sabbath means to the life of a family. To two-year-old Aryeh, Shabbat is, "Daddy. Shul. Home." No wonder this day is acknowledged weekly in some sort of observance at every Jewish school, and why each child we spoke with had an answer to the question, "What is the Sabbath?"

What is the Sabbath and what do Jewish people do on that day?

Sabbath is the seventh day of the week. We rest because God rested when He was creating the world.

Benji, age 9

We go to synagogue, eat lunch and have play dates.

Nina, age 7

Sabbath is the seventh day of the week and the most holy day of the week. It's to remind us that God rested and we should, too.

Allie, age 12

God said everyone should take the day off, like He did.

Timothy, age 8

They light candles and eat challah because God rested after creating the world.

Samantha, age 7

We keep Shabbat because, if we didn't keep Shabbat, God wouldn't let us have Friday. My favorite part of Shabbat is dessert.

Yehudit, age 4

On Shabbat you don't have to work, because God worked for six days and on the seventh day He stopped. First He made cheese. He also made cats and flowers and lions and the light and He also made people and the water and the sky and the birds.

Rachel, age 5

On the seventh day, Hashem rested and He told all the Jews to rest. Before that He was making light and dark.

Lizzie, age 4

It means we have to go to the synagogue to pray.

Rachel, age 4

Shabbat is a holiday we have every week. It's a day of rest. God rested from making everything.

Gila, age 7

We have Shabbat because God wants us to drink wine. It's a time when we pray at night and in the morning. It starts Friday night at six and ends Saturday night at six.

Morgan, age 8

We have Shabbat to celebrate that God made the world.

Marty, age 4

God rested after making the world. God made bugs, fish, worms, people, trees, fruits and vegetables. Since then He also made appliances that help Him make more stuff. He keeps creating more people and more people and grass and seeds so everything can keep starting over again.

Sara, age 7

Shabbat is a holy day when there is no school and I can sleep in.

Kaley, age 10

Well, we're the only part of our family in Waco who's Jewish, so we just usually go to synagogue and spend it with each other.

Lacey, age 12

It's when grown-ups drink wine.

Brian, age 9

Shabbat is Daddy. Shul. Home.

Aryeh, age 2

We have the Sabbath so we can sleep.

Esther, age 8

On Shabbat, we light candles because on the seventh day God created candles.

Adiel, age 4

The old rabbis thought that Shabbat was the most important day and I agree with them because that was the only day God got to rest.

Mark, age 5

6

The Jewish Calendar, Part II:
Holy Days, Holidays and Festive Times

The rhythm of Jewish life is punctuated throughout the year by holy days and holidays both solemn and joyous, a cycle of observances commemorating Judaism's historical heritage and spiritual imperative. Each holiday has its scent, its spice, its set of customs and even clothing. Each has its lessons, and its symbols and observances to stamp them indelibly in children's imaginations.

In the fall, camp ends, school begins and it's time to buy new shoes and pick out shiny red apples to place on the dinner table alongside the honey for the traditional sweet greeting of Rosh Hashanah, the Jewish New Year. During this time, reflections on the year before, and focus on becoming better souls in the year to come, prompt some families to observe the Tashlich tradition of going to a body of flowing water to symbolically toss away last year's sins so they may start the new year with a clean slate.

Zach's family did so one Rosh Hashanah afternoon. But, that night at dinner, the four-year-old could not stop acting up. When his actions finally resulted in a glass of wine spilling over the tablecloth, Zach became serious. "I think I'd better go back to that place by the river," he said.

Soon after comes Yom Kippur, a day most children will spend in synagogue alongside their parents, who, fasting and reflecting, may be less fun than usual. Yom Kippur is rarely a favorite day for children—or adults. But it's a time of introspection, and even the youngest among the children we spoke to were able to focus on something in their behavior they would like to improve upon. A week later comes the harvest holiday of Succot, when small booths are erected outside synagogues and homes to accommodate the custom of eating in these huts for the duration of the holiday, recalling the dwellings of the ancient Israelites during their post-exodus wanderings. Children make decorations and enjoy the adventure of comparing themselves to the Israelites in the desert.

The final day of the Succot holiday has a special title—Sh'mini Atzeret, which marks the intimate lingering before the final good-bye at the end of the Holy Day season. On this day, Jews pray for rain to be brought on the wings of angels during the coming fall season. With dusk comes Simchat Torah, among the happiest days on the Jewish calendar. Meaning, literally, rejoicing in the Torah, the last chapter of this great book is read, the scroll rolled up, and then unrolled to begin the year-round cycle of readings again. Each child who comes to synagogue receives a paper flag or toy Torah along with treats of apples and candy, and the atmosphere of prayer and awe that marked the previous weeks gives way to singing and dancing.

A few weeks later, of course, comes Hanukkah, the highlight of the year for so many children, the favorite of nearly all, and justifiably so. Not only are there presents, but eight nights of candlelight, crisp latkes (potato pancakes), plays, concerts and games of driedel.

Tu B'Shvat, the birthday of the trees, comes in the depth of winter, a harbinger of spring. Traditionally celebrated by planting trees in Israel and eating dates, carob and other fruits of that land, Tu B'Shvat has grown in importance to children in recent years with the surge in environmental consciousness. Indeed, this once minor observance has become the favorite holiday of many children for whom the appreciation of nature is strong.

Then comes Purim, with the reading of the Megillah's story of how Queen Esther and Mordechai saved the Jews from the decree of wicked Haman. Celebrated by dressing in costume, giving gifts of food to friends and donations to the poor, along with a sumptuous feast, Purim nudges Hanukkah for "best holiday" honors among children.

"Shushan's gone," said Zev, age 3, as he marched into school the day after Purim and noticed immediately that the poster depicting the ancient city described in the Queen Esther's Megillah was no longer hanging on the hall. He slipped into a classroom decorated with Passover symbols to hear his teacher reading the story of Moses. "Let my people go," said Zev. At this holiday, the most elaborately ritualistic of all, it's the home, not the synagogue, that is the center of activity. Guests and family gather to hear the Haggadah, the story of freedom from slavery. The meal consists of symbols such as the saltwater of slavery's tears, eggs of eternity and the unleavened matzah that substitutes for the flattened bread the Jews did not have time to bake completely during the hasty flight from Egypt.

There are also foods that make Passover Passover—family recipes for fish and soup without which the holiday would not be complete. Grandparents stay overnight; cousins fly in; there are prizes for hiding and finding the Afikomen—the broken piece of matzah served for dessert. This ancient custom was devised to keep the children interested in the seder narration, to enable them to fulfill the commandment that every Jew in every generation should feel as if they themselves were freed from Egypt.

That's a powerful image that lasts well beyond the seder night, as Sam's mother learned months after Passover. "Jacob," she heard her five-year-old ask his younger brother. "Do you remember when you were a slave?" Or there was Katie, who was bored and disappointed one day when none of her friends were available to play. Her mother suggested she use her imagination. A few minutes later the seven-year-old was seen solemnly walking out the front door with downcast eyes. Mother asked what she'd decided to do. "I'm going outside to pretend to be a Jew wandering in the wilderness," answered Katie. And finally, there was Oran, who, at age 4, gave this blessing to his parents each week at their Shabbat table: "I bless you that you should come out of Egypt."

Next comes Shavuot, commemorating the giving of the Torah. It's a lovely, almost pastoral, holiday, celebrated with nurturing symbols of dairy foods. This commemoration of Sinai was the favorite of nine-year-old Mark, for instance, who couldn't think of a more "important" occasion in Jewish history, "along with the blintzes and cheesecake we eat then, of course." People engage in all night Torah study on this holiday and pray at dawn.

And according to a legend popular among children, the sky is said to open at midnight, and all things wished for seem all the more possible. In one family, the parents met on Shavuot, precisely at the midnight hour, a story that has long intrigued their children. Since their youngest days the children have asked to be woken up and carried outside to view the celestial portal.

With summertime comes the dramatic story of Tisha B'Av and the destruction of the Holy Temple and the dispersion of the Jews. The Lamentations of Tisha B'Av are often read at night, the story followed along with candles or flashlights in darkened chapels or alongside the mountain lakes and rivers of summer camp, recalling the long ago rivers of Babylon, "where we sat and wept for Zion."

And then, the circle turns again to Rosh Hashanah and renewal.

With so many holidays and so many traditions associated with each, it's a wonder children keep them straight, but they do, more or less, as we found out when we asked them these questions about the Jewish holidays.

What is Rosh Hashanah and how do Jewish people observe it?

Rosh Hashanah is the head of the year.

Sam, age 8

Rosh Hashanah is a holiday of judgment and God judges us to see if we will have a good year or not. We dip apples in honey, to have a sweet year, and I play with my cousins when they come.

Benji, age 9

On Rosh Hashanah, we throw bread in the water and ask God to forgive our sins.

Nina, age 7

On Rosh Hashanah, we start fresh with a new slate, like a baby does when they are born. We pray, eat big meals and get together with family.

Allie, age 12

On Rosh Hashanah, we speak in Hebrew.

Cort, age 8

On Rosh Hashanah, we go to Minneapolis and see our cousins. We have a sweet new year and eat apples and honey.

Grace, age 7

It's the holiday that you dip the apple in the honey.

Rachel, age 4

On Rosh Hashanah, we dip the apple in the money.

Elana, age 3

We see our families, and grown-ups don't eat.

Madeline, age 5

It's a new year for the Israelites.

Martin, age 10

Rosh Hashanah is when we say Happy New Year to people.

Rebecca, age 5

We go to people's houses and eat stuffing.

Max, age 5

Rosh Hashanah is a holiday when the Jewish people got out of Egypt.

Eddie, age 5

On Rosh Hashanah, we blow the shofar. We eat honey so the year will be sweet. I wish that people won't do bad things and that bad things won't happen.

Matt, age 9

At Rosh Hashanah and Yom Kippur we talk to God about the year before and what we would do differently in the New Year. What would you talk to God about?

In the New Year, I will feed my pussycats crunchies and wet food and I will also give them fresh water. I will clean up my Legos and my blocks all by myself.

Lawrence, age 4

I'll play nicely with my brother Michael and clean up my room.

Rachel, age 4

I would want to get better grades and do better at spelling,

Max, age 8

They have to have special children's services on Rosh Hashanah because it's so important—they make sure we're there.

Darryl, age 9

I want a Discman and I hope my family stays healthy. I will try not to procrastinate and exercise three days a week.

Benji, age 9

I would want more freeness in the world and for all the bad guys to be good guys.

Robbie, age 8

I ask for a good year and that there won't be another world war. I usually don't give new year's resolutions, but each year I try to be nicer to people than I was the year before, and it works. I have different resolutions for the Jewish new year and the English new year, like the Jewish new year is more about my character, and the English one is how I could do better in school and things like that.

Avishai, age 10

I want to start over again, to try to be a better person, do better in school and be more organized.

Allie, age 12

You learn from your mistakes in the past year and try not to do them again.

Adam, age 8

It's the beginning of our year. It's great to have a time when everything starts over.

Liora, age 10

I want to be better in first grade than I was in kindergarten because I got pretty much time outs in kindergarten.

Richard, age 5

I am going to help Mommy cook dinner.

Gabriella, age 4

In the new year, I'd like to get more sleep.

Carrie, age 9

I would like to see the Spice Girls.

Morgan, age 8

I ask that everyone should be healthy.

Lauren, age 7

I will wash all the dishes and crack all the eggs.

Richard, 4

We say we are sorry to ourselves and we promise we'll never do bad stuff again. When I get mad at my brother, I'll talk to him and not hit him.

Grace, age 4

We pray for forgiveness for our sins and tell everyone we're sorry for what we did wrong.

Martin, age 10

I would like for us to have a good year, and all the years after that. That means I would hope good stuff would happen in our family and that no one in our family dies, or that a friend of our family or of my parents dies, and I hope God writes my name on a good list.

Sara Noa, age 7

I would like to do better stuff and help people more.

Sherri, age 7

I wish people that their year will be better than their last year. I wish that I will get presents.

Elan, age 7

Passover, Purim and all the others

In our congregation, people get really into all the holidays. If there's a holiday coming up, we stop everything we're doing in Sunday school and make decorations. On Hanukkah, my mom came down to the synagogue and cooked latkes for three hours straight. Even if it's one of the less important holidays we make it into a big bash. I love how my congregation gets into it.

Lacey, age 12

On Passover, we do all kinds of things, like eat bitter herbs to make us feel like the Jews felt when they were slaves. We're supposed to feel suffering.

Emily, age 5

On Passover, we celebrate that the Jews were free because if that story didn't happen we would still be slaves in Egypt and I would not want to be a slave.

Helen, age 5

Passover is when you can't eat any more food.

Lizzie, age 4

On Passover, you are supposed to feel like you were a slave in Egypt and know how it felt to suffer, so when I made my

Hagadah in school I drew a picture of when I got a paper cut because that made me really know what it feels like to suffer.

Rebecca, age 5

You can't eat bread on Passover because it's not good for you.

Max, age 4

Passover is a happy holiday to celebrate when the Jews escaped from slavery.

Danit, age 8

On Purim, we wear costumes because Esther's name means hidden, and Esther hid that she was a Jew and pretended to be something else so we dress up in costumes so we can be hidden and no one knows who we are.

Sara Noa, age 7

Purim is a Halloween for Jews.

Jonathan, age 11

Purim tells about Haman. Haman was hung the same way Jesus was hung.

Rebecca, age 12

Haman was being really loud, so on Purim, we shake graggers to make noise to remind us about Haman.

Maital, age 4

On Purim, we read the Megillah and shake goggles.

Chana, age 3

On Purim we use maracas for noisemakers and we make hamentashen.

Zachary, age 4

On Simchat Torah, we read the Torah, eat challah and drink apple juice. On Purim, we dress up in costumes and say boo to Haman.

Morgan, age 8

On Yom Kippur, we ask God to forgive us for everything we did.
Avishai, age 10

On Yom Kippur, I try to fast because it helps you concentrate on praying. I think about how many people died in the past, throughout history, like in the Holocaust and Anne Frank.
Liora, age 10

Sukkot we build a succah because God wants us to eat outside.
Lauren, age 7

On Simchat Torah, we finish reading the Torah and start reading it all over again because there's always new stuff coming into your mind and each time you read it you get at least ten different new ideas, and the rabbis usually say something different about each chapter. Well, some rabbis.
Noa, age 8

We celebrate Simchat Torah because of when the first Torah was written.
Brian, age 9

Tu B'Shvat is very important. It's the birthday of the trees. When my daddy doesn't have fruit to put in his fruit store, he goes to the trees to get some, and if there were no trees, there would be no fruit for Daddy to sell, only vegetables.
Richard, age 4

On Passover, we celebrate the ten plagues of Moses.
Cort, age 8

What do you know about Hanukkah?

Hanukkah is about the bad king Antiochus. But not all kings are bad. There was Martin Luther King Jr.
Rebecca, age 6

We light the menorah and get lots of wonderful presents.
Benji, age 9

We light candles for eight days of Hanukkah because the oil lasted for eight days.

Morgan, age 8

We light candles and sing songs in front of the window so everyone can see our family.

Allie, age 12

When I found out Hanukkah was not in the Torah, I was angry. I told my mother to call the rabbi who writes Torahs to put it in.

Jonathan, age 5

We eat latkes and we light the menorah because the Hebrews didn't have much oil to light the menorah. They only had enough to last for one night and it lasted for nine days. They rebuilt the holy temple but they couldn't find any oil.

Lauren, age 7

The Jews were in the desert and they needed oil to last eight days.

Daniel, age 11

Hanukkah is about Antiochus, who was this mean king, and his bullies ruined the Temple, so the menorah tricked Antiochus by burning for eight days.

Maital, age 4

I know it's important to celebrate Hanukkah and Purim to remember the people in the Bible, because if they didn't do what they did then we wouldn't be free today.

Samantha, age 7

Hanukkah comes from Disney.

Bill, age 3

On Hanukkah, people eat turkey and give each other presents.

Brent, age 4

The most important part of Hanukkah is that we don't pray to idols anymore. Some people thought that God was in idols.

Richard, age 5

It's when we celebrate about a war when we were saved from an evil king who didn't want the Jews to do their stuff.

Anna, age 7

In my house, first we light the menorah; then after that we open presents, and after that we eat dinner, and after that we play dreidel, and after that we find the matzah for five bucks.

Cort, age 8

Hanukkah is when we play dreidel, which is the game the Jews played when they were slaves in Egypt one hundred years ago.

Shelly, age 6

Hanukkah is about people being brave and sticking up for what they believe in. Sometimes I have to do that in school and the story inspires me to be brave.

Samantha, age 11

The story of Hanukkah is about giving the people food and presents. The oil lasted eight days.

Max, age 5

It's about the Jews, and if we didn't have the Maccabees, we wouldn't have Hanukkah.

Madeline, age 5

It's about oil and menorahs.

Grace, age 7

On Hanukkah, we light the menorah, sing "Dreidel, Dreidel, Dreidel" and watch Hanukkah tapes.

Benny, age 5

What is your favorite holiday?

Hanukkah, because we get presents.

Peninah, age 4

Hanukkah, because you get presents. I got a real camera.

David, age 5

Hanukkah, because of the presents.

Jack, age 11

I like Hanukkah, because my mom is really big on charity; so each year, during one night of Hanukkah, we go to a toy store and we find something we would really like, not something we think someone ought to like, and we give it to someone less fortunate than us. Instead of having eight nights of presents, it makes it really interesting.

Lacey, age 12

Shavuot because it's the holiday when we got the Torah, which is the most precious thing in Judaism. And you get to eat cheesecake, which is tasty.

Daniel, age 10

Friday night at our synagogue is a pretty special time. I feel the presence of God is there. Shavuot is my favorite holiday. I feel closest to getting the Torah then.

Davidi, age 12

Purim, because I like to get dressed up and deliver shalach manot (presents of food) to people.

Allie, age 12

I like all the holidays the same because we have lots of fun on the holidays.

Sara, age 7

I like Passover, because I get a prize for finding the matzah.

Michael, age 6

I like all the holidays because I get to see my cousins.

Shawn, age 9

I like the holidays because I spend them with Mommy, Abba and my brother and everyone in the whole world who is my friend.

Rachel, age 4

Hanukkah. I like lighting the menorah and remembering the miracle of Hanukkah. *And* I like getting presents.

Benji, age 9

I like Passover because you get to taste all these different foods and you get to spend time with your family.

Rebecca, age 8

Purim. You get to dress up, and even though the first day of Purim starts with fasting, you get to eat a lot on the night of Purim, and my shul always has a carnival, which I love.

Avishai, age 10

I like Purim because you get to have a lot of candy, you bring shalach manot to people and you get some, too, and you get to go out in the streets in costume, and because it's a happy holiday.

Danit, age 8

I like Passover because of the food, and we all get together at my grandparents' house, all the family, and we hide the afikoman and it's just a lot of fun.

Natalie, age 11

Passover, because we get to go to my grandmother's and I love the seder. On Hanukkah, I like to light the menorah, play dreidel and get gelt. On Purim, I like to dress up, like as a Reese's Cup.

Becca, age 6

Shabbos because I get to be with my family, and I get to go to people's houses and have friends come over. I also like Pesach (Passover) because if you find the afikoman you get a prize.

Ariella, age 6

My favorite is Passover because I get to see my great-grandma and my grandma makes matzah ball soup—the *best!*

Rebecca, age 12

Hanukkah, because I like looking into the candle flames in the menorah. It's mysterious.

Ronnie, age 11

Passover, because the night before you go to California, you play a game called cleaning the house. You use a candle and a feather to find crumbs.

Donni, age 4

I like Passover because I like all the food, and I like reading out of the Hagaddah. I also like Shabbat, but I especially like it at camp because that's the time I get to talk with all my friends.

Daniel, age 12

I like Succot and eating in the succah, having guests over and getting compliments on the food. I love Sh'mini Atzeret, because it comes at the end of all these serious holidays right before we start the year over. It's a fun holiday, you get candy, and it's just the kind of boost you need to have a head start in starting your year in a fun way, not a sad way.

Liora, age 10

Passover, because I love matzah ball soup, and I love the afikoman hunt, and all the food, and it's just so fun with all the family being together. I also love Hanukkah because normally you're off school on break and there's presents and the menorah and stuff.

Jonathan, age 11

I like Hanukkah because you get presents. But you can't get a Christmas tree or decorate the outside of your home with lights.

Grace, age 7

I have lots of favorite holidays but I like Rosh Hashanah because sometimes I go to my grandmother's, and at her synagogue there's a big room to play.

Chai, age 6

I like Rosh Hashanah because it's a happy time, and I like Hanukkah because we light candles and get to eat chocolate Hanukkah gelt.

Meir, age 4

Passover, because it's my birthday time.

Esther, age 6

My favorite is Purim because of the yummy hamentashen.

Yosef, age 4

I like Tu B'shvat because that's when we celebrate the birthday of the trees and trees give us paper, wood for building, homes for animals. They make the world beautiful and God created them, and if it wasn't for trees, there wouldn't be other living things.

Naomi, age 6

Most people say Hanukkah because of the presents, but I don't care much about that. I like Passover because there are so many celebrations with family. The seder is a good experience to hear the story, even if you don't know the Jewish language.

Jake, age 9

What do Jewish people eat on holidays?

On Hanukkah, we eat latkes to remember the miracle of the oil. We eat them with apple sauce and sour cream because it tastes good. On Passover, we eat Matzah and everything on the seder plate. Matzah is a hard bread because when the Jews were leaving Egypt they didn't have time to let the bread rise and it became hard. We also eat grapes, figs, dates, olives, carob and pomegranates.

Benji, age 9

On Passover, we eat matzah, because when we were slaves leaving the desert, Pharaoh said that you can go and quickly we had to bake some bread, and we didn't have enough time, so we took it out of the oven before it rose.

Esther, age 6

On Shabbat, Jewish people use grape juice for wine.

Grace, age 4

On Passover, we eat parsley and vinegar.

Brian, age 8

On Shabbat, we eat challah because it's a special bread. That's because in the old days farmers were not able to eat good bread. They had to eat bad bread, except for on Saturday when they ate bread made with eggs.

Ellie, age 7

On Passover, we eat matzahs because you don't bake them with flour so they don't rise because they didn't have enough flour to bake bread.

Morgan, age 8

On Purim, we eat these cookies that look like Haman's hat. What are they called? Omelets?

Martin, age 10

Hard-boiled eggs, eggs dipped in saltwater and all kinds of eggs.

Aviva, age 6

Latkes and haroset.

Martin, age 9

Eggs and tears.

Mali, age 4

On Hanukkah, we eat latkes and chocolate money.

Benny, age 5

We eat matzah on Passover because they didn't have enough time to bake it fully on their trip because they knew the Pharoah and his army would be coming at them and try killing them; so they only took five minutes baking it and it was flat bread so they just packed it up and left to the Dead Sea, which Moses split in half so they could go through and when Pharoah and his army came through they all died.

Martin, age 10

On Passover, we eat hard-boiled eggs and this kind of stuffing. I forget its name. And we eat those roots with saltwater.

Cort, age 8

On Hanukkah, we eat doughnuts with jelly.

Morgan, age 8

Parsley and eggs.

Zev, age 3

We eat hamentashen, but I don't know why we eat the hat of a bad man.

Gavi, age 4

What other foods do Jewish people eat?

Chicken soup.

Eytan, age 11

Chicken.

Max, age 5

Matzah ball soup.

David, age 11

Fish in carrots. And kosher jerky.

Martin, age 10

Kosher.

Nina, age 7

They eat no wild animals or animals that eat other animals and no fish without scales and fins.

Ariella, age 7

Horseradish.

Cort, age 8

Lollipops from Mr. Bender.

Zev, age 3

Jewish people learn how to catch fish and eat them.

Grace, age 4

Noodles with cheese.

Peninah, age 4

Do you know what food God does not like? God does not like deviled eggs.

Becca, age 6

Tuna, rye bread with seeds, challah and chicken.

Simeon, age 11

Roast beef.

Ron, age 11

Whales and dolphins aren't kosher. But they *are* very friendly.

Sam, age 4

Stuffed cabbage.

Jesse, age 11

Felafel.

Saryah, age 10

It's not fair that nonkosher people get to eat kosher and we don't get to eat nonkosher. It's also not fair that in Israel, a place full of Jews, people don't even know what kosher pickles are.

Kaley, age 10

Sour cream.

Rachel, age 4

Knaidlach.

Zoe, age 6

Jewish people eat good food and kosher food and apples and oranges and cookies and watermelon and grape juice and wine and challah and bananas.

Rachel, age 4

7

Angels, Miracles and Wonders

Rebecca marched into the shoe store down her block and looked around. "Yep. Raphael is here," she announced, reassured.

"Who is Raphael?" asked the salesman.

"That's the angel who sleeps at my feet, so Raphael can help me pick out shoes."

"Oh, I see him," answered the salesman. "He's right over here."

"Oh, no. That's not him. *She's* over there."

Mom explained: Each night, Rebecca's father sings her a song about the angels who watch over her from every direction as she sleeps. She's a little off on this angel's traditional perspective, but when you're a four-year-old lying in bed, it's hard to point to "behind" without motioning to the feet.

Other angels are welcomed into Jewish homes as special guests for Sabbath with the singing of the famous hymn "Sholom Aleichem" on Friday night. Are Jewish children filled with wonder and belief in miracles? Do angels guide their lives? Children are prepared for anything, and why not? Each one has opened the front door to let the prophet Elijah into the house to sip wine from a filled glass at their seder table, when an uncle or aunt usually shakes the table a bit underneath to make sure the children witness the "sip."

Many children have learned the story that complete knowledge of Torah is taught by the angels to each baby in heaven, prior to birth, only to be removed in the moment before birth by the angel's touch. That gentle touch, which legend says causes the indent above their lips, is why children have to spend so much time in school trying to get that knowledge back. That's why Shira was in Hebrew school, the six-year-old explained.

Each child has experienced something miraculous. A shiny dime conveniently appears on the way to the ice cream store or a fly ball obscured by a blinding sun makes its way into the center of a baseball mitt. Miracles can happen. And angels are present— though, for Jewish children, they're as often manifested as the spirit of someone's beloved "Bubbie" (grandmother) as they are the agents of God in more traditional theology.

What is a miracle?

A miracle is when we prayed for my baby brother to come out of the hospital when he was sick, and he did.

Sarah, age 7

A miracle is something that in real life couldn't happen, but when you really, really need it, it happens.

Gila, age 7

A miracle is like on Passover when God split the sea. In most of the wars in the Bible, the Jews win. When the Jews were traveling through the desert, God gave us lots of special stuff.

Caren, age 8

A miracle is like when the water split and God sent the ten plagues. Miracles are things that only happened a really long time ago.

Ariella, age 6

A miracle is when the Red Sea opened and all of Pharaoh's men drowned and stayed under water for one hundred years.

Chai, age 6

Do you believe in miracles? Are there miracles that happen in the world today?

Do I believe in miracles? Yes. Y-E-S! Because I believe in God and God makes miracles and I have proof. When my cousin was born, I went to the hospital and saw some babies that were born too small. They had to stay in a tank for a while with lots of tubes coming out of them so they could breathe. I'm glad I wasn't born like that. But then they could come out and live. Also, if there was a war and you lived through it, that's a miracle, like my grandmother was in the war, and she's alive and I'm thankful to God for that.

Sara Noa, age 7

A miracle today is when you wake up every day being normal, not having a tumor, not being sick, and being able to go to school. It's not always the big things that count as miracles. It's the little things.

Lenore, age 11

I believe in miracles, but they happen very rarely. A miracle in this day is that Israel has survived through all the things it's been put through, and the fact that Israel is there at all is a miracle on its own.

Avishai, age 10

We don't have miracles like the story of Hanukkah and the oil lasting eight days and all anymore. A miracle today is like if I got to be the star in the school play.

Jill, age 9

I don't know if I believe in miracles, because nothing has ever really happened.

Marla, 8

I believe in miracles, but I don't know why.

Leah, age 6

There are plenty of miracles in the world today. It's a miracle you're breathing. Scientists have tried to make a small piece of us, like make a model of an organ, and have it work the way it does in our body, but they can't make them so small the way they are inside humans. It's just amazing the way we work, the way we think, how we know how to make things. People think that a miracle is when voices come out of the sky or fire. That could happen, but really, what's normal is a miracle.

Aliza, age 10

A miracle is like when Mommy finds the ketchup, and my brother gets cuter every day.

Rivka, age 6

I wouldn't exactly call what happens today miracles, but good things happen, like we get to go to the park, even when it's cold outside, but sometimes it's a beautiful, sunny day, and also lucky things happen.

Talia, age 7

A miracle is that every day me and my brothers fight but that no one has ever gotten really hurt. A miracle is that you wake up every morning. It's a miracle when people get out of things alive. You hear about car crashes and stuff all the time if it's big enough to be on the radio, but people get out alive. It's a miracle that we had a fire in our house and everyone got out alive.

Liora, age 10

Let's say there's a robber and he stole everything you have, and he ran away to Japan or something, and they found him and you got everything back. That's a miracle.

Molly, age 9

A miracle would be like if it snowed and there wasn't school and then it snowed and snowed and snowed and all the buildings would be covered and there still wasn't school.

Alexandra, age 6

A miracle would be if maybe a kid lost a tooth on Christmas or Hanukkah and they got extra presents. That would be really special.

Sherry, age 8

A miracle would be if everybody was rich.

Allana, age 6

A miracle would be if all the Jewish people wouldn't have to do Jewish stuff.

Mark, age 9

If kids never had to go to school.

Miriam, age 8

If a kid lost three teeth at once.

Mikey, age 5

If everyone got free medical insurance.

David, age 8

People don't notice miracles as much today. There are no big things like the Red Sea parting, and people don't really watch for miracles. They just happen every day.

Joey, age 11

Do you believe in angels? What do angels do?

Angels do all different things. Some of them wipe your tears.

Dassi, age 5

Angels collect the mitzvas (good deeds) that people do.

Ariella, age 6

You don't really know what angels look like. People claim they see them, but it could be a regular person. If I saw an angel I think I'd ask, "Why didn't Moshiach come yet?"

Aliza, age 10

Angels pray for people.

Richard, age 5

Angels are there to help God help you out.

Naama, age 13

People walk around and have angels leading them in the right direction.

Esti, age 13

I think when somebody dies if their soul is brought to God and found to be perfect they get to turn into angels and help everyone else be perfect.

Leeya, age 13

Yes, I believe in angels. It's when someone very close to you dies and then they are watching you, and they're with you and they watch where you step. Like my grandmother.

Ronit, age 6

Angels bring miracles to Jewish people.

Samantha, age 7

The angel who watches you is somebody who is exactly like you. They have a matching personality.

Gilit, age 12

I guess there are angels. You always hear about them. There are more Jews today than ever before, so there must be more Jewish angels.

Rebecca, age 8

I hear about them all the time. I can't really say if I believe in them or not, but Elijah the prophet is like an angel. He shows up when people are in trouble, but he never leaves footsteps.

Liora, age 10

Angels carry messages from God. I believe in them, but not that they come down to earth.

Avishai, age 10

An angel is like a double of you. They know everything about you.

Sara, age 12

I think there's an angel watching everybody. What if you're just walking along. You could just fall into a gutter and you wouldn't see it. An angel can make a pathway for you wherever you walk.

Davidi, age 12

If an angel came to your house, what would you ask the angel to do?

If an angel came to my house on Sabbath, I would ask it to help me set the table.

Brendan, age 7

I would be really happy if an angel came and helped me clean up my room.

Anna, age 7

I would not ask for anything specific.

Yosef, age 4

If an angel came to my house and we were in a fight, an angel would come in and break up the fight.

Samantha, age 7

I would like it if an angel played with me in the sand.

Lawrence, age 4

I would say, "I love you."

Rachel, age 5

I would like to go look for seashells with an angel.

Lauren, age 4

I would give it presents.

Richard, age 4

8

Rabbis, Synagogues and Prayer

Mrs. Greenstein's nursery school class was brought to the temple's main sanctuary just days before Rosh Hashanah. The rabbi was scheduled to help introduce the children to the ceremonial objects that could be found there. Into the sanctuary he strode, dressed in the flowing white robe he would wear on the High Holy Days. The children's fidgeting stopped and there was a hush. Then came the whispers from one to another: "Look. There's God."

Rabbis can be awesome figures, or they can be "the guy who tells us Torah stories," as eight-year-old Rebecca described. And synagogues can be boring places. Or they can be just great. Much of that depends upon whether the child has to sit quietly next to his or her parents and listen to the rabbi's sermon, or whether there are scheduled activities, someone to narrate the week's Torah story, or a "candy man"—the kind, older adult found in synagogues throughout the world whose pockets are loaded with lollipops, sweetening the Sabbath experience. Little children, most of whom have never even walked around the block by themselves, somehow navigate their way through the forest of tall people in the pews to find the candy man, who reinforces the idea that religion is supposed to be, at least for children, a generous and gentle place. It was for Jake, even at eighteen months. As his parents pushed his stroller closer to the Manhattan temple they attend, one famous for its liturgical music, Jake would point to the building. "Singing?" he asked, instead of synagogue. Parents go to the synagogue to pray, children to play and pray. What do people do when they pray, and what do children pray for? From a Barbie doll to world peace, prayer is something personal to children, and heartily felt.

What is a rabbi?

The rabbi is the one who reads from the Torah in the synagogue.
Ariella, age 6

A rabbi speaks at the shul, he teaches Torah and he helps people, but not a whole lot.
Dassi, age 5

He's the one who helps everybody pray. He's also a teacher.
Anna, age 7

The rabbi is the person living in God's house.
Grace, age 4

The rabbi blows that big thing, the shofar, on Rosh Hashanah.
Rachel, age 4

He helps you learn things.
Christopher, age 8

Rabbis know other rabbis and rabbis talk to other rabbis.
Zachary, age 5

The rabbi takes on more religious responsibility. He takes his job very seriously.
Davidi, age 12

The rabbi tells stories about the Torah when you go to the synagogue.
Danit, age 8

The rabbi is the person in the shul.

Yosef, age 4

Our rabbi is the guy who gives hugs to you on Shabbat. You go to him to look things up, to learn things. He's a teacher, he keeps history going, he reads the Torah and gives the blessings.

Liora, age 10

If you go to the synagogue on Shabbat, the rabbi says the Shabbat prayers.

Rebecca, age 8

The rabbi is basically the leader of the shul, or at least one of them. He's a very holy person and kind of a leader in general.

Avishai, age 10

What do people do in the synagogue?

People pray and read the Torah. I play.

Benji, age 9

I pray to God, go to Sunday school and dance.

Max, age 5

We pray for the Maccabees.

Maddie, age 5

We pray and say hi to God.

Grace, age 4

People pray and listen to the—what's it called? Rabbi? I sleep.

Martin, age 9

My mother always gives me the Bible and I think to myself in secret, *What am I supposed to do with it?*

Brooke, age 10

People go there because it's a nice place to visit because it's

God's home. I go there to pray. I ask forgiveness from God. I pray for no war.

Cort, age 8

Abba and Mommy daven. I tell my Daddy I want to go somewhere else in the shul.

Rachel, age 4

They thank God for their food and drink.

Anna, age 7

You talk to God and you speak Hebrew. People pray for their dead.

Lauren, age 7

I bother my mom.

Morgan, age 8

Sometimes on Shabbat, I stay in the whole time, but sometimes it's to impress my parents.

Liora, age 10

I play and eat candy.

Hila, age 4

My parents count the kipahs and hats on people. I twiddle my thumbs.

Marla, age 8

I pray for love and kindness and respect and friendship. And more Gameboy games.

Morgan, age 8

They pray and sit on chairs. You also learn not to cut the Torah in half, and not to cut the rabbi's head off.

Ephraim, age 5

The grown-ups talk to God about King Pharaoh and wish that he would get flushed into the Nile River.

Dan, age 4

The candy man gives me candy. Sometimes two candies.

Donni, age 4

They pinch my cheek because I'm cute.

Ethan, age 9

People go to synagogue so they could pray to God. Some people do it because they'll get a good life in the next world, or if not, God will punish them some way. Some people do it because they love God and want to thank him and ask him for a few requests.

Kaley, age 10

I play in the playground.

Erica, age 6

I'm just starting to come to the synagogue more. When I was younger, I would just sit around and be bored, but now I try to think about praying.

Jackie, age 11

What does it mean to pray?

I close my eyes when I pray to God, because God is like a great big sun. When I hear the music when people pray, it's like God is smiling at me.

Tamar, age 5

You say you're sorry for things you've done and hope for things to happen.

Timothy, age 8

To pray means you are thanking God for breakfast, lunch and dinner. Jewish people pray to thank God. If they did something wrong, they ask for forgiveness and try to be a better person. I pray for the things I need and for my safety and health and other people's health.

Benji, age 9

People pray because they want to thank God and sometimes they hope for something or they are afraid.

Anna, age 7

It means to thank God and praise God.

Allie, age 12

When you pray, sometimes you think you hear a response, but God doesn't understand the human language. Maybe there's another language God understands, like body language or telepathy. When you have a good feeling about something, I think maybe He or She—that's how I refer to God—puts that feeling into you.

Josh, age 11

It means to thank God for all that He did and ask that nothing bad happens.

Avishai, age 10

Basically, prayer is when you keep trying and trying to talk to God. If you hear a response, you probably already knew the answer before, and you think God puts it into you.

Adam, age 11

People pray to ask forgiveness from God and they want to bless people.

Cort, age 8

It means to say to God we want a new baby. People pray because they want a baby.

Rachel, age 4

To pray means to speak to God and thank Him for things. If you're a grown-up, you can pray for a baby.

Moriah, age 6

People pray because they want the rest of the world to be caring and kind. Sometimes they pray to their dead grandparents.

Morgan, age 8

To pray means to say things to God, like to say what you hope will happen in your life.

Joseph, age 9

We pray to God because He makes everything we have. Inventors make stuff, but God gives them all the things to make it with, so things keep getting made.

Sara Noa, age 7

To pray means to ask God for things and thank God for things in a special holy language.

Simon, age 10

To talk with God. Jewish people pray to ask for good.

Zohar, age 6

What do you pray for?

I pray for peace in the world.

Miriam, age 8

I pray for a house.

Gila, age 7

For the Yankees to win.

Timothy, age 8

When I say a bracha (a blessing) it's to ask God if I can eat something. I would pray that God would build the Beit Ha'Mikdash (the Holy Temple) for the Jews.

Shlomiyah, age 4

I pray that poor people won't starve.

Ariana, age 6

I think about what I'm saying and what the words mean. When I say the blessing after meals I keep in mind my family.

Bruria, age 12

I would pray to God to come and play with me.

Richard, age 4

If someone is sick, I pray for them to get better. If someone is mad at me, I pray they won't be angry.

Allie, age 12

There's a part in the prayers where you get to pray for whatever you want. In that part I pray for people who are sick to get well, to get really, really better. Also, I lost my retainer, and it's not really important like other things, but it's really embarrassing, so now I pray I'll find it.

Liora, age 10

I want to learn to ice-skate and visit my grandmother in Israel.

Anna, age 7

I talk to God about saving people.

Hila, age 4

I try to say the Sh'ma whenever I remember. At different times, I pray for different things. Today is my Mom's birthday, so I would ask that she have a happy day. I'm on the basketball team at school, so maybe sometimes I'd ask that my team would win. I hope to get a good job, and I'd like to get into the University of Pennsylvania because a lot of people in my family went there.

Jacob, age 12

When I can't make up my mind I ask God for help so I know what to do, like go to someone's house for a play date or stay with my family.

Moriah, age 6

I don't ask God for anything, because so far, I have pretty much everything I need.

Yosef, age 4

I would ask God to make my mother not be allergic to cats so we could get a cat.

Shawn, age 9

I would ask God to teach me about fishing.

Grace, age 4

I would ask God to cure everyone so that no one should be sick. I think He would tell me to do more commandments and to learn more so that I can understand them.

Davidi, age 12

We pray for people who gave up their lives just for you, like Martin Luther King Jr.

Samantha, age 7

If something really bad happens, I would ask God to make it not happen.

Brendan, age 7

I would ask God to teach me ice-skating.

Rachel, age 5

9

Mitzvot—The Pursuit of Good Deeds

"When I am twenty-one, I would be rich. I would gamble and smoke cigars. I would have all the cars in the world. I would give homeless people homes and money. I would give kids toys and a good education. I would get people off the streets. I would rebuild temples and churches. And I will be nice." So promises Judy, age 10.

Along with almost every snack a parent packs to Hebrew or Sunday school goes a penny or more for tzedakah (charity), a can of soup for the food drive, or hats for a homeless shelter. Doing a mitzvah literally means to do one of God's commandments; mitzvot (plural) can comprise the many acts of kindness people can do, no matter how young. Whether it's helping set the table, putting away toys or collecting books for needy children, for some children doing mitzvot defines their Jewishness.

What are some of the things they do to help others? And how does doing a mitzvah make them feel?

What is a mitzvah?
What kind of mitzvahs do you do?

A mitzvah is saving friends from bullies, even if you don't want to.
Zachary, age 4

It means going out of your way to do the littlest thing to any living thing and feeling good about it. My bat mitzvah is coming up and I'm going to give some of my bat mitzvah money to tzedaka.

Lacey, age 12

It's visiting somebody when they're sick.

Lizzie, age 4

A mitzvah shows you care about people.

David, age 5

A mitzvah is when you do something good for other people, you do something good for yourself, for teachers or other people at school, or for dogs, or animals or any living thing. When I was three, I fell into the middle of my swimming pool and my aunt jumped in and saved me. That was a mitzvah from her to me.

Arielle, age 9

A mitzvah is to clean up your toys, and it's nice to let other people play with your toys.

Ayelet, age 4

A mitzvah is when you let people color on other people's pictures.

Rivka, age 5

If you translate it, they are commandments. You do good things because it's a commandment.

Rebecca, age 12

A mitzvah is when you give poor people money and food and medicine. That's what you learn about when you're Jewish.

Richie, age 5

Other religions do good things in different ways. For us, mitzvahs are part of being Jewish. Like, at my synagogue, you participate in a mitzvah project, like making sandwiches for poor people. I like it. It's a good idea.

Jack, age 12

A mitzvah is when you become a man.

Brian, age 9

It's helping people make things they don't know how to make.

Donni, age 4

What mitzvahs do you do?
How do you feel when you do them?

I make cards for people, I invite Grandma and Grandpa to my school play and I help Grandma walk. I give charity because poor people don't have money. When I give charity I feel wonderful.

Nina, age 7

I do all the mitzvahs that I can do. I give old clothes to the Salvation Army.

Allie, age 12

I like giving charity. That's something Jews do. It's what makes me Jewish, and it makes me feel special.

Jill, age 9

We gave charity to help our friend get better when he was in the hospital.

Kali, age 4

I feel relieved, because I've helped somebody so that takes away from some of the bad stuff I've done.

Ben, age 12

A lot of people don't have homes. I feel proud when I help them.

Emily, age 7

I go and visit my great-grandmother because she doesn't get out much and I also end up playing bingo with all these old people.

Rebecca, age 12

We give tzedaka because some Jewish people don't have food

and clothes and shoes. I feel I want to give more clothes, more food and more shoes.

Rachel, age 4

It means doing good things, which I try to do all the time. I try to be nice to people whenever I can, but when somebody gets on my nerves . . .

Samantha, age 9

One time I heard a really big yell in our backyard and we saved this woman who was stuck out on her balcony on the top floor of these apartments, and she gave us all ten dollars, and it was so cool.

Jonathan, age 11

Over the Christmas holiday, we bought toys for kids and put them under the Christmas tree at a place for abused and neglected kids.

Ricky, age 9

My grandpa's sister is in a nursing home and we go visit her. And my great-grandmother is like ninety-four now and every night my dad calls her and talks to her.

Kalize, age 11

There are people who don't have the things that we do. If the Torah has pity on them, you know it's an important mitzvah to give charity.

Avishai, age 10

You know how there are lots of poor people in Israel? I saw them when I went there with my family. Well, I was going into a restaurant with my parents and these two poor people wanted shekels. I tried not to let my tears come out, but they did, so my mother let me go out and give them money.

Natasha, age 7

My aunt was in the Holocaust. She was in hiding with her mother in this house, but once a Jew came to the door and begged for food, and my aunt gave it to him, and her mother yelled at her because then they didn't have food. We always hear that story in my family and it makes me feel proud.

Tali, age 8

Doing mitzvahs makes me feel proud of myself, and it shows an example.

Harry, age 9

I would give food to old, poor people and help them out with things they don't know how to do.

Brendan, age 7

I go to shul and I pray, and I go visit my grandparents, and I respect my mom and dad most of the time and I respect my sister a little bit of the time.

Natalie, age 11

10

Marking Time Jewishly: Life Cycle Events

Boys won't remember the day of their brit milah, or bris, when they were eight-day-old babies being circumcised and entering the Jewish covenant. Girls won't remember the day of their simchat bat—a ceremony literally meaning "happiness for the daughter"—when girls are welcomed into the community of Jews. But parents would do well to take pictures, or save a souvenir from those times, for as children grow and see others, including baby brothers and sisters experiencing these rites of passage, they'll want to know what happened when they were born.

They have some ideas, as Kaley, age 10, demonstrated when she said, "I know why Jewish baby girls come out happier than baby boys. They know they won't have a bris."

Emma, at her sister's simchat bat, wanted to know if her parents were "happy" when she, too, was born. Luckily, the parents had saved a script of the blessings of the day, strung together with lace binding, to show how happy they indeed were.

By the time boys near the age of thirteen and bar mitzvah, and girls age twelve and bat mitzvah, they are well aware that the occasion means more than a party. Religious obligations are involved, and sometimes family ones as well, even if it's the younger sibling's turn to start treating the bar or bat mitzvah with proper deference. That was Davey's expectation as he neared his big day. "On my bar mitzvah, I'll read the Torah, have a party and tell Jackie he better start listening to me more."

Whether it means coming to synagogue regularly from then on, or writing thank-you notes for all those presents, every Jewish adult knows a bar or bat mitzvah is a day they will never forget.

When a baby is born Jewish people have a ceremony—a bris for boys, and sometimes a baby naming for girls. What happens at a bris?

At a bris, they dip a baby's pacifier in wine.

Nina, age 7

At my brother's bris they cut the stem and left two strawberries.

Miriam, age 3

A bris . . . Uh-oh. I know, but I better not say.

Ariana, age 6

I know what it is. It's gross, and it's not for girls. I don't want to say it.

Morgan, age 8

A bris or a baby naming for a girl is a celebration when you have a baby because Jewish people like to celebrate things like that.

Nechama, age 7

A bris is a time when babies don't have fun.

Jonathan, age 11

At a bris someone gets a baby.

Lizzie, age 4

What is a bar or bat mitzvah?

A bat mitzvah means that I am going to be responsible to myself and responsible for what God expects of me.

Bruriah, age 12

It's when a boy turns into a grown man. Like in the movie *Jack*. He's a boy in a man's body.

Cort, age 8

A bar and bat mitzvah is to celebrate when a boy or girl becomes a man or woman.

Allie, age 12

A bar mitzvah is a right of passage into manhood. I don't know if I'll feel more like a man overnight after my bar mitzvah, but it's better than not having something to mark becoming a man.

Alex, age 12

A bat mitzvah is the beginning of an older life.

Rebecca, age 11

A bar or bat mitzvah is when you celebrate that a son or daughter is becoming a man or woman. They have more laws to follow, but that's a sign of growing up.

Ronit, age 6

Most non-Jewish kids think that having a bar or bat mitzvah is *sooo* cool. You have a big party, get money and presents. They look at the religious part as something boring and meaningless. But to Jews, it means more than all the money in the world, even if they won't admit it.

Sophie, age 12

My sister's bat mitzvah means that she is growing up and acting more like an adult. Usually people say an adult is age eighteen and up, but in the Jewish religion, when you're thirteen, you are becoming an adult and you have to be more responsible, even though you're only a young teen.

Ariel, age 10

To me a bat mitzvah is like a fresh start in life. You get a chance to change yourself, and become a different person if you want. You're maturing. I'm a very active person. Nothing is going to change that, but other things are already changing for me, like

I'm getting more advantages and more responsibilities, like we got a dog, and now that I'm older, I take care of her more.

Jenna, age 11

It's when you reach a certain age you become an adult in your Judaism. Even if you just gave a speech, I think God makes something happen inside you.

Lena, age 11

After your bar or bat mitzvah, your parents trust you more.

Gary, age 11

A bar mitzvah is when you have to stay in shul and you can't play.

Ephraim, age 5

A bar mitzvah is when I become a man kind of. I have to pre-pare a lot for it, but it's worth it not just for the party but it feels like it's really being Jewish. All the boys in my family are older than me and they've already been bar mitzvah. After my bar mitzvah, I'll feel like I'm one of them.

Jacob, age 12

A bar mitzvah is a reward for learning all this stuff. It's a level of maturity. In some cultures, people say you're mature when you're eighteen, but you don't get a big ceremony then. It's when you understand things more, you realize stuff on your own and you can be more by yourself.

Josh, age 11

11

The Jewish Family:
Honor Thy ... Grandparents

Hardly a grandmother today can be found bound to her
kitchen, cooking pots of soup, baking kugel or challahs for
"when the grandchildren come." Nor will Grandpa be waiting at
home to spin stories of when he was a child. More often than not,
Grandma will be driving her Civic to take her granddaughter to
the Gap or basketball practice, and unless she's like twelve-year-
old Esti's grandma "who always overcooks," the supper she
spreads out upon returning home will likely be totally fat-free.

Grandfather, meanwhile, will be researching the Internet to
send, via E-mail, the reams of material he thinks will help the kids
with their homework.

But since both Mom and Dad are tied up at work today,
Grandmother and Grandfather will often be the ones with time
to fill in as audiences at the Purim play, listen to countless recita-
tions of the "aleph bet" or to help review the bar or bat mitzvah
portion. Some grandparents can still remember their own parents' immigrant experience, and there are some who survived the
Holocaust or took part in the founding of the state of Israel.
They make good interview subjects for school reports, and their
experiences bring home the reality of both the tragedies and tri-
umphs of Jewish history.

Some children may never have had the privilege of meeting
their grandparents, but they understand how much these ancestors

continue to be a part of their lives. After the bris of her little
brother, who was named after his two deceased grandfathers,
four-year-old Sara Noa observed, "Life is like a long story that
never ends. God just puts in new people. First our family had
Zeyde and Abba. Then Daddy and Mommy. Then Abba and
Zeyde died and we got Zev." Her biggest wish today? "That
Moshiach will come so I can meet Zeyde and Abba."

The Jewish people are known in the vernacular as the Sons and
Daughters of Israel (an alternate name for Jacob), despite the fact
that Abraham and Isaac precede Jacob as patriarchs. Explained the
famous twentieth-century scholar Rabbi Avraham Solevetchik,
Jacob was the first of the patriarchs to have a relationship not only
with his children, but with his grandchildren as well. It is with
Jacob's blessing to his grandchildren, Ephraim and Menashe, that
Jewish parents bless their children on the sabbath. So essential to
Judiasm is the transmittal of tradition across generational lines,
that the people's own descendency is linked to Jacob, rather than
his father or grandfather, whose biblical relationships are not as
transcendant. It's no wonder, then, that the bond between grandparents and grandchildren is strong. Each is a source of pride to
the other. Grandchildren light up their grandparents' world. And
when children are asked about the texture and flavor of Jewish
family life, they say it's the gransparents who "add the spice."

Jewish life often revolves around the family.
How do relatives, like grandparents and others
outside of your immediate family,
add to your Jewish life?

My grandfather always calls before Shabbat and asks questions
about the Torah portion for the week. He sang a Yiddish song at my
bat mitzvah. My grandmother always overcooks when we come
there—meatballs and chicken. Grandparents are always there for you.
Esti, age 13

My grandfather tells us it was hard to be Jewish when he was a
kid. It was hard on Shabbat because you couldn't drive to synagogue. It was too far away. And sometimes he was treated badly.
Jon, age 10

My grandparents are so proud to see that their children's children are learning about being Jewish that it's an honor to keep up being Jewish. In a way they didn't get to experience their own childhood, especially if they went through the Holocaust, so they're happy to see the kids being happy.

Sara, age 12

When my grandfather was young, on Shabbat all he could do was read. There was nobody around to be with. He was very poor and his parents had to work very hard, so he had to do the chores. Now he's happy our family is Jewish and we can afford more than he could, and we have friends to be with on Shabbat.

Daniel, age 10

My grandfather was in the army in the war and he helped free Jews. I feel proud of him.

Yaron, age 10

My great-aunts went through the Holocaust, and they look at things from a different perspective. When I hear about their experiences, I feel I can have the same experience they have without having to go through what they did. My great-grandfather also wrote down his whole life story for us before he died. It's amazing to see what he went through. You learn a lot from older relatives.

Aliza, age 10

Since Grandma Judy died, she talks to me in my head. She gives me good advice.

Emma, age 7

I was really close to my grandmother, and after she died I would sometimes talk to her at night. I would ask her questions or ask that she help us out with our problems. I thought I could hear her answering. I would insert her name in my prayers every day.

Sara, age 12

I go to my grandparents' house to relax.

Leeya, age 13

My grandmother arrives at our house for Passover a day before the holiday and her knuckles are cut and cracked from cooking all the food she brings.

Sarah, age 12

Your grandparents are the ones who add the spice of being Jewish into your life. When I go there for Shabbos, it's just so much fun. They help form you Jewishly. They know things from the past about being Jewish, and as soon as you walk into their home, it's like that atmosphere surrounds you. In a sense, they're more righteous than your parents. They have a way of teaching you without yelling at you. It's like they're teamed up with angels. Especially in our generation, after the Holocaust, they appreciate seeing life continuing. If you read history books, you think everything is so far away, it won't effect us. But if you're connected with your grandparents you are more connected to that history, and you can see how everything effects you, too.

Emily, age 12

Grandparents do things that parents don't always have time to do.

Naama, age 12

Grandparents might tell you more about being Jewish, or they tell you the correct way to do things to be Jewish, more than your parents do. My grandparents are in Florida, but they come to us on Passover.

Rebecca, age 7

My grandmother ran away from Hitler when the Nazis came, so I feel good she got away. My grandfather helps me with the Jewish letters.

Anna, age 7

Your grandparents connect you with your background and family customs.

Elisheva, age 12

Grandparents are sometimes better at things than your parents. They're more experienced. And they give you extra attention.

Sara, age 13

12

Israel

Accessible as an airplane trip, distant as ancient history, Israel holds a place of utmost importance in the education of Jewish children. Money is collected at school to plant trees in Israel, and images of its stone-hewn architecture, its deserts and mountains and its blue-and-white flag are familiar to all.

But unless a family has traveled there, and even if they have, the reality of a modern land upon which the stories of the Bible were played out is sometimes hard to absorb. "It's a warm place. It's very important to the Jewish people, and many of your grandparents go there," the rabbi at Charlotte's preschool told her class. "Do you know what place that is?" "Florida?" came the four-year-old's response.

Gali, age 4, noticed that everything in Israel seemed to be Jewish. On a family outing to the Ein Gedi nature preserve, she observed the area's goats, those legendary animals of biblical prose. As the creatures gamboled across the sand-covered desert stones their stiff, scraggly beards stood out in profile. "Are these Hasidic goats?" she asked.

What is Israel? "It is louder," said one second grader. "It is further away," said another. "It is hot and people speak Hebrew."

"It smells of hamburger and soda," according to one young pilgrim.

Still, Israel is inspiring. The country's music stirs emotions on annual Independence Day celebrations. Older cousins travel there for school and volunteer service. And the word "homeland" enters early into a child's vocabulary. No matter what part of the globe they live in, or whether they live in Israel itself, the fact that the eyes of the Jewish world turn there so frequently establishes for children a sense of connectedness with something beyond their street, their city, their school, to a society that stems from those ancient forebearers whose footsteps still echo. Is Israel important to Jewish children? Just listen.

What and where is Israel and what does it mean to the Jewish people?

Israel is the Jewish homeland in the Middle East. It's important because out of all the nations, God picked the Jews to give them the Torah and their homeland was Israel.

Allie, age 12

Israel is a holy land for the Jews because God gave it to us. It's a nice place for Jewish people to live. I sent a letter to be put in the wall from the Temple there. It was one of the walls that didn't break down because it was glued together with love. All the other walls of the Temple were built by builders but this wall was made by the people themselves.

Gila, age 7

Israel is our homeland and it's where we live. Our Lord promised it to us, and our forefathers are buried there and they were our leaders. It's where a lot of people like to pray and where the Temples were destroyed.

Daniel, age 12

Israel is the land God sent the Jews to after they left Egypt. It was a land of milk and honey. It's a holy land.

Allen, age 9

Is it in Jacksontown? Or near it?

Lauren, age 7

It's where Moses brought the people from slavery and they call it the land of milk and honey.

Natalie, age 11

Israel is a place for everybody. It's a place to make us all close to

God. It's a place for all people, but it's a place where Jews can flourish.

Aliza, age 10

That's the place where God led Moses to. But he did something bad, so God let him see it but not go in. It's a place where the Jews went to go free, and most of the population is Jewish, but there are a lot of Christians there, too. Also, it's hotter.

Natasha, age 7

It's where all the Jews settled after moving away from every country until they came to that place and it started to become a monument of Jews. Moses died on the way there when the people were crossing the desert.

Martin, age 10

More people smoke in Israel than in America. The Jews speak Hebrew and the Arabs there speak Hebrew, too. Israel is important because it has all those mummies and statues from a long time ago that are important to the Jews.

Katherine, age 7

It's in the fertile crescent.

Halyn, age 12

It's the land God gave to us for the Jewish people to survive.

Rebecca, age 12

Israel is basically where all the Jewish people come from. Without Israel, Jewish people will have no origin.

Ronit, age 6

It's where Moses led them after a 50-year journey.

Morgan, age 10

It's between Asia and Africa and it's in Europe. It's important to Jews because the Temple stood there and the Kotel (the Western Wall) still stands there, and that's a very important landmark in Jewish history. Israel is important because it's a pretty good place for the Jewish people or the Hebrews. It's important because people can talk their language over there and it's really a good tourist town. It's safe but not that safe because they don't have peace in some of the surrounding countries.

Jonathan, age 11

It seems like a great place where a lot of things are good, but I know there's also a lot of bad things, like bombs and things. It's sort of like the Torah is alive there, you can see everything that went on, but it's not just in writing. It's actually there.

Jacob, age 12

It's important because a lot of Israel's victories happened there, the whole Jewish culture happened there and God promised it to Abraham, Isaac and Jacob. It's also where I get souvenirs.

Liora, age 10

That's where the two temples were. I think that Jewish people suspect that everyone in the past lived in what is now called Israel, and maybe everyone, from Adam and Eve on, spoke what is now called Hebrew.

Jerry, age 11

It's our nation, our place.

Saryah, age 10

It's the center of Judaism and all the other religions respect our religion the way we respect theirs because Israel is there.

Yitz, age 10

Israel is shared by all the Jewish people.

Alan, age 12

It's in the Middle East and it has cities like Haifa and Jerusalem. It's the land of milk and honey.

Anna, age 7

It's where a lot of Jews live and it's got so many Jewish things.

Kalize, age 11

It's a small place that doesn't have a lot of states but it's in the city of Jerusalem and there's a desert there and it used to be really big, but now it's smaller.

Chai, age 6

13

Of Hanukkah, Christmas and Interfaith Relations

Sam made a new friend in his new neighborhood, and the friend invited him for a sleepover on a Saturday night. "Okay, Roger. I'd like that. I'll come over after Havdalah," said Sam, referring to the ceremony with which the Sabbath ends. "What?" asked Roger, confused. "Wait a minute," said Sam. "Does your family celebrate Hanukkah and Passover, or Christmas and Easter?" "Christmas and Easter," came the reply. "Okay, then I'll come over when it's dark."

Jewish children have many ways of defining themselves in a world in which they're a minority. In Jonathan's case, the world was divided according to which holidays one observes. Sometimes, going to Hebrew school instead of band practice after school is where the difference lies. For other children, food is an identifying factor, especially if a family keeps kosher. Gila, for one, the only child in her public school's second grade who eats only kosher food, takes pride in the name her classmates call her: "Kosher Girl," she says with pride. "Because I check the packages of everything we eat at parties and stuff to see if there's a kosher sign. I like when they call me that."

For other children, a best friend from a different faith enriches the experience of Jewish observance. "I like when Cathy sleeps over and I get to explain about the mezuzah on my bedroom door, and the candlesticks and all the Jewish things we have," said seven-year-old Dara.

Today's generation of Jewish children growing up in America will not likely produce a body of secular literature akin to that of the generations before, when Judaism's clash with the larger culture was often central to a literary plot. Jewish children today have the video validation of the *Rugrats* gang celebrating Passover; and Moses himself became a superhero, a "Prince of Egypt" of animated cinematic proportion—perhaps the ultimate cultural blessing in many a Jewish child's world.

Volumes have been written on the subject of the Jew in a gentile world, particularly during winter, when the confluence of Christmas and Hanukkah has even earned itself the name of a syndrome: "The December Dilemma." The dilemma is one for Jewish parents and educators worried about the attractive pull of public squares and shopping centers glowingly decorated for Christmas, and the barrage of television specials and commercials that build up the anticipation of a holiday of unimaginable excitement.

The dilemma is clearly there for many Jewish children, who found it necessary to describe the differences between the way both events are celebrated when the subject of holidays in general came up. But in listening to children, the focus is less that of concern than comparison. Only a few children expressed sadness, that their teachers said only, "Merry Christmas," instead of "Happy Hanukkah," on the day before winter break, or that the Hanukkah decorations seemed to come down too early. Sarah's father learned an important lesson from his five-year-old daughter one December night. Driving through a park festooned with trees lit up for Christmas, Dad noticed the little girl looking at the lights. As a cantor at a synagogue, he had been dealing, throughout the day, with the issue of Christmas and Jewish identity and how seductive it is to kids, how parents can end up feeling like the Grinch. As they drove through the trees, Sarah said, "Oh, Dad. What beautiful things the Christians have done." "She got it," he observed. "It is beautiful. And it is not ours. And that is fine."

None of the children we spoke to, though, would have chosen to observe a holiday other than Hanukkah during that time of year. In fact, said many, eight days of Hanukkah instead of one day of Christmas? More time to see all the cousins, eat more latkes and get more presents.

When the rabbi at Eli's synagogue asked what was the greatest gift God gave to the Jewish people, he was thinking of the Torah; one four-year-old proved the centrality of this holiday by shouting out for all to hear, "Chocolate money!"

Concerning Hanukkah, Christmas and other interfaith matters . . .

We wouldn't get presents on Hanukkah if it wasn't for Christmas. Christmas came around the time of Hanukkah and some Jewish kids said, "I wish we could get presents," so one family started giving presents and then lots of families started it, too.

Sarah, age 7

I'm Jewish. Are you Christmas?

Ben, age 7

Avi was three when his mother took him to a local shopping mall on a Friday afternoon. They were waiting on a bench in the mall eating their ice cream, and Mom noticed Avi looking intently at the scene of children lined up to sit on the lap of Santa Claus. As they were leaving the mall, Avi suddenly stopped and said: "I'll be right back." He ran over to the display where Santa Claus was sitting, and as Mom ran after him, she heard him yell at the top of his lungs, "Santa, Santa." Everyone in line stopped to look at this three-year-old who then yelled, "Shabbat Shalom (Good Sabbath), Santa!"

If one of your friends are Christian and you go to church with them, you can go but you can't kneel. Also, if you have friends who are Christians, you should be nice and even though you celebrate two different kinds of holidays, you should invite them over and share your presents.

Nora, age 7

Shoshana was about ten when she began wondering how non-Jewish adults find out there isn't a Santa Claus since they grow up being told by their parents that Santa is real. After all, at some point you have to learn to buy Christmas presents for your children and pretend they are from Santa. She thought about this for a long time and finally came up with the answer. As you are being wheeled into the delivery room to give birth to your first baby, that's when your parents tell you Santa isn't real.

I'm glad I'm not non-Jewish, because when you get ten presents a night for the twelve days of Christmas, you get really spoiled.

Abby, age 7

Avraham's family was out for a drive one December evening. As the family drove past a creche on a front lawn, the four-year-old observed, "Look, there's Judah Maccabee and his family."

When Isabel was four she asked whether Santa was coming to her house. Her mother carefully explained that little Christian boys and girls believe in Santa. A few months later, Isabel wondered if the Easter Bunny was expected. Again, Mom explained that Easter was a Christian holiday and that Jewish children did not celebrate it. Finally, the little California girl asked, "Do little Christian boys and girls have snow?"

I feel good about being a Jew. Half of my family are Christians and we all get along together. Everyone's friends because there are no wars anymore against the Jews.

Daisy, age 9

Genevieve, age 5, loved watching President Clinton on TV. One day during the holiday season she asked, "Isn't that Hanukkah Lewinsky's friend?"

A week or two before Hanukkah, Sydney, age 5, was in the car with her mother, driving past all the homes decorated with colored lights for Christmas. "It's not fair. Everyone is getting ready for Christmas, and no one is ready for Hanukkah."

Four-year-old Alexandra was discussing the religious background of her grandparents. One set is Jewish and one is Catholic. "I know," she said. "Grandma and Poppa are Jewish and Grandma and Grandpa are California."

When Ari was nine, his mother overheard him making fun of his friend Chris for still believing in Santa Claus. Mom took her son aside and said, "Do you still believe that Elijah comes to every Jewish house on Passover night and takes a sip of wine?" "Of course!" he replied. And then he said, "Oh, I get it."

Yori's mother bought him a new suit jacket for Shabbat. It had a Christian Dior label. "Can I wear this?" the eight-year-old asked.

Lisa's pre-K class was interviewed for a TV show. Lisa, age 4, was asked, "Do you believe in Santa Claus." As a good Jewish girl, she replied emphatically, "No!" Then she was asked if she believed in the Easter Bunny. An aficionado of rabbits, Lisa replied, "Of course!"

We celebrate different holidays and I think we're more serious. We don't have bunnies that bring us eggs, or a guy in a red suit. It's not like I'm sad about it, but the teachers don't make a big deal about the Jewish holidays. When you think of the holidays, everyone thinks of Christmas.

Perry, age 12

14

On Being Jewish Today

Children in Jewish schools and Jewish families are instructed to "be a good Jew." They work with its language and expressions and sometimes make do with expressions of their own. They also have definite thoughts about their existence as Jews, feelings that emerge in response to questions, in observations that captivate their parents and teachers and in stories that make raising Jewish children the delightful, rewarding challenge it has always been and continues to be today.

What does it mean to be a good Jew?

To do everything your Mommy and Daddy say.

Nina, age 7

To love and believe in God and *try* to follow the commandments.

Allie, age 12

It means you do all the right things, follow the Torah and be the best you can be.

Benji, age 9

It's a person who serves God instead of cussing at Him, and saying I don't have to listen to Him, You're not real, You're fake, or I hate You, like Jonah did. Jonah did *not* really listen to God.

Martin, age 10

It means to be kind to other people and not to do mean things.

Matt, age 8

It means to do good deeds, like plant a tree on Tu B'shvat.

Andy, age 6

To follow every tradition and every law.

Ronit, age 6

A good Jew is someone who prays every time they go to services, does all the Ten Commandments, is loyal to God, and doesn't cuss not one single word and he's nice to each other.

Morgan, age 8

What do you like or not like about being Jewish?

I like going to a Jewish school.

Nina, age 7

I like learning a different language, like Hebrew. That's the Jewish language.

Sarah, age 5

The holidays, the people and the schools.

Allie, age 12

I like going to Temple on Saturday. And I like going to Hebrew school.

Benji, age 9

I like everything, except Hebrew school.

Stephanie, age 9

I like all the holidays because that's when we see our cousins upstate.

Ben, age 9

I don't like that we have all these traditions and laws because since there are so many sometimes I can't avoid breaking them.

Ronit, age 6

If I was Catholic, I'd probably say I like being Catholic, but I like Judaism because it sort of gives you a choice of what you can do and not do.

Josh, age 11

It's just the way I like to be.

Brendan, age 7

I like that on Friday I never get homework because of Shabbat.

Abbey, age 6

I like being Jewish because our religion is not so strict, and you can choose to be strict or not.

Adam, age 11

I like being Jewish because it's the way you naturally look at something and we have a real close relationship to God and it's just an exciting life to live.

Lacey, age 12

My favorite thing is being happy and being nice to my friends because that's what God said to do. You also get all these great holidays. I also like being Jewish because I like being myself.

Anna, age 7

First of all, I like being Jewish because it's like being different than most of the other kids at school, and when they have questions, I'm really happy to answer them because it's so different from what they know, and also because on the holidays you get to spend time with your family and there's good food, and when you pray you're praying to God and you have special events like bar and bat mitzvahs when you get to be counted in the minyan.

It seems like every year there is one kid who is *soooo* interested in our religion and so interested in bar mitzvahs and Hebrew. They call me Bat Mitzvah Girl.

Natalie, age 11

Sometimes I feel uncomfortable if I walk into some place and not everyone is Jewish and my brothers are acting up. You don't want them to do that because people will look at you and notice you're Jewish.

Liora, age 10

It's nice to be different than most people who are Christian. Also, we read all the biblical stories and there are all these Jewish people who are really good and I think it's just neat to know you're the same religion as these people who saved a thousand people.

Mikka, age 10

I feel kind of special because some people have been hurt in my religion, like in the Holocaust, but I'm not responsible for hurting other people in other religions.

Jenna, age 11

I like being one of the oldest religions.

Halyn, age 12

Sometimes it's hard to be Jewish when you see people eating things you can't eat and driving around on Shabbat when you can't.

Peter, age 11

I think it's cool to have people in your family from all different places and times. That's something Jews have. Like my grandfather. He's from the Holocaust.

Bryan, age 9

I like going to synagogue with my mom and hear Abba (the rabbi) pray.

Rami, age 5

I like everything—the holidays, the food. I think it's really unique. I think being Jewish is a special gift that God has given me so that I could live in a Jewish community, even though there's just two temples in Waco.

Samantha, age 9

It has its advantages. It has its disadvantages. It has a few rules, but some of the Jewish rules that are in Israel aren't the same as in America.

Kaley, age 10

I like being Jewish because Jewish people are on the good side of things.

Geoff, age 4

There are a lot of holidays and that means you can spend more time with your family.

Marla, age 8

I like everything. I think our language is neat, our food. I think we're just lucky to be who we are.

Arielle, age 9

What I don't like is me and Martin are like the only two Jewish kids in my whole school. The other kids see my (Hebrew) books and say "What *is* this? This isn't handwriting. This isn't anything." And I told 'em it's Hebrew. It's what Jews read.

Morgan, age 8

What I like about being Jewish is being free. I do not like knowing that we used to be slaves. I don't like that we do not have many Jewish songs. And we don't have a Jewish channel.

Martin, age 10

I think some other religions are too commercial. I like being Jewish because it's not commercial.

Evan, age 9

I like when my mommy makes challah for Shabbat.

Eli, age 5

It's fun because you celebrate Hanukkah.

Max, age 5

I think it's a special gift, and it's a very special gift to me. I'm not going to cover up for that. I like all the holidays we celebrate and I like explaining them to my friends. Sometimes it gets annoying, explaining about keeping kosher. And I like meeting other Jewish friends. There are so many of them.

Jonathan, age 11

I like the language Hebrew, and I really like learning it.

Daniel, age 12

We get to have Hanukkah, because I like getting presents. I like drawing stars. I don't like to go to Sunday school.

Shoshana, age 5

I like being Jewish because every time there's a holiday, there's no school. My mom lets us dip apples in honey.

Noah, age 7

I like being Jewish because my mother and father don't have to work on Saturday.

Ariella, age 6

My favorite thing is we have more holidays than if you're not Jewish.

Johnny, age 5

I like being Jewish because it's different. It's not like everybody else. In our school there's one hundred fifty kids in my grade and maybe five or six are Jewish. It's a completely different religion and it's a great gift to be Jewish. It was given to us by our ancestors, but it's not like I wouldn't want to be Jewish anyway. It's a cool religion, and even I'm interested in it when I explain it to my friends. That makes me feel like they want to know more about other things than only their religion and other things out there. But it's kind of sad that we don't have as many Jews after the Holocaust.

Rebecca, age 12

How do you say . . . ?

My dad got a new car! It's a super Jew car!
> *Judy, age 6,* on the family's new Subaru

We give thanks to Todd for bread.
> *Jacob, age 4*

Why did Haman want to keep all the juice?
> *Tamar, age 3,* on the Purim story
> in which Haman vows to kill all the Jews

Esther does not like Ayin.
> *Esther, age 2,* on learning the Hebrew alphabet
> and confusing the letter "Ayin" with "onion"

God created the animals, the plants, everything. He is God of the University.
> *Micha, age 4*

Shana Tova. Happy New York.
> *Rafi, age 3*

Aleph, bet, Gimbels . . .
> *Natalie, age 4*

Eliyahu's on TV . . .
> *David, age 3,* singing the
> Passover song "Eliyahu HaNavi"

I Don't Know Lam.
> *Lisa, age 2,* singing the popular hymn
> "Adon Olam" (Lord of the World)

15

A Question for a Question

Old joke though it may be that a Jew answers a question with a question, and has a story for every story, Jewish children of today proved that this is no exaggerated cliche. Every discussion of Jewish observance, history and belief provoked dozens of questions. Many had to do with the origin of God; all were penetrating, perceptive and imbued with insight. A year's worth of school curriculum material, or subjects for rabbi's sermons, were contained within, as children posed conundrums that have stumped scholars for centuries. So from the children, the their questions—and their last words—on being Jewish in the world today.

What questions do you *have about Judaism or being Jewish?*

Are all old people Jewish?

Rebecca, age 4

On Yom Kippur, I tell God everything I did wrong. But who does God talk to?

Israel, age 5

The Children of Israel got the Torah, right? And they built the Ark and all that other stuff. And they fought the battle of Jericho. So what were the grown-ups doing all this time?

Joey, age 7

How old do I have to be when I can stop keeping Shabbat?

Adam, age 11

Why does God do all these things to Pharaoh in the Passover story? I mean, why did He have to have ten plagues instead of one plague? It's like He was showing off that He was better than Pharaoh, and God isn't supposed to show off. And why did God make Pharaoh bad anyway? If he wasn't bad, the Jews wouldn't have been slaves in the first place.

Becky, age 6

I wonder why people used to hurt the Jews a really long time ago, and also they said the Jews were really bad. That makes me feel bad.

Naomi, age 8

Why did all snakes have to slither forever after the snake made Eve eat the apple? Why didn't God punish just that one snake?

Sara, age 7

Why were Adam and Eve born as grown-ups? They had a shorter life than if they had started out as babies, and if they were the first people God ever made, wouldn't He want them to go through their whole life?

Becca, age 6

Weren't the two tablets too heavy for Moses to carry?

Elana, age 6

If God doesn't have a body, then He doesn't grow, right? Then He's like Peter Pan, right?

Sam, age 5

How did God make Himself? How was He always there?

Nechama, age 7

When God writes in the book of life at Rosh Hashanah, is God writing in cursive or printing?

Micah, age 8

Are there Jewish robbers and do they work on Shabbat?

Ilana, age 6

God created light, and He created all the animals, and foods, and trees. But how could God make all those things if He doesn't have hands?

Claire, age 3

I know where babies come from, but where do Jewish babies come from?

Michael, age 6

If God made the bees and the seas did He make the A's and all the other letters, too?

Elana, age 4

Why can't God make people stop killing people?

Alex, age 8

Why can't God make world peace to open the seventh gate of heaven?

David, age 9

How come God doesn't speak to people anymore?

Talia, age 7

Is Barney the Dinosaur Jewish?

Jenny, age 3

How can we eat ham and tashen if we can't eat ham?

Etan, age 5

Did Rebecca ever see Rachel? I mean, she sent a messenger to find a wife for her son Isaac and he found Rachel, so did they ever get to meet? Also, did Elijah really climb up a ladder to heaven?

Rebecca, age 8

Why is the synagogue we go to, Beth Shalom, named after my sister instead of me, Ilana Shalom?

Ilana, age 3

If Jews are the chosen people, why are there so many Christians?
Mikaela, age 7

Am I a prince, because David was our ancestor, and he was king of the Jews?

Kyle, age 8

How much is infinity, because God has been around infinity years, and how was God created anyway?

Andrea, age 8

Why did Moses stay up there so long on the mountain?
Danit, age 8

When mommies and kids are angels, will they recognize each other?

Etan, age 6

How did God grow up without parents? And where was God before He was born?

Haviva, age 3

Can God create the dinosaurs again? I think He should.
Sammy, age 5

When Moshiach comes, and everyone returns to life, how will my soul know which body is mine?

Chaim, age 7

Some stories shared with us

A Sunday school teacher brought her "magic bag" full of Shabbat ritual items to class. She let the children take the objects out of the bag to touch them. Scott, age 5, was grasping the kiddish cup. "What is the kiddish cup used for?" the teacher asked. "It's the cup used only for kids," answered Scott.

Eli's doting uncle asked if his six-year-old nephew would like to come live with him in Boston. "We have day schools in Boston, so you could go to a Jewish school," offered the uncle to his observant nephew. "You think I'd be religious if I didn't live with them?" said Eli, pointing to his parents.

A young cantor prepared her children's choir for the concert that was to be their temple debut. Scott, age 8, was enthusiastic. "You know what I love about singing in Hebrew? You can sing and clear your throat at the same time." .

A class of second graders was learning the Chumash, the Bible text in Hebrew. The Hebrew word for daughters—*banot*—and for bananas—*bananot*—sound somewhat similar. Thus, translated one child when reading about Lot, "And Lot took his two bananas and went out of Sodom."

Kendra's father was studying the biblical text concerning the creation of the world, and he read to his twelve-year-old daughter the story of the creation of mankind and the Garden of Eden. When Dad read the "flesh of my flesh" part, Kendra asked for an explanation. Later on in the day Kendra was misbehaving, prompting her father to ask where she got this bad behavior. "Flesh of my flesh, bone of my bonehead," shot back the preteen.

Barbie dolls were not allowed in Rachel's home when she was very little, because her parents believed the doll's message was about how she looked rather than what the character could do. One day when Rachel was seven, the family was eating at a fast food restaurant and the "Happy Meal" came with either a toy car or a tiny Barbie. Mom decided that Rachel was old enough to choose for herself. She picked the doll, saying she was going to call it Rabbi Barbie.

Three-year-old Chaja, watching a news show about the pope and his cardinals leading a service in St. Peter in Rome, asked, "Are they Jewish?" When the reply was no, she insisted, "They must be. They all wear kippot."

"My favorite Jewish game is cops and robbers, because throughout history someone was always chasing us," said Kaley, age 10.

Nicholas's mother was reading him a book about Hanukkah and wondering whether the story was sinking in. "And why didn't the Jews want the statue of Zeus in the temple?" she probed. "Because he was a made-up character, like Santa Claus," Nicholas explained.

A week or so after Hanukkah, Mindi was driving past a synagogue that had had a flea market the week before and still had up the balloons that had served as decoration. "Look, Mommy! Balloons!" shouted three-year-old Jonathan. "Why do you think they're there?" asked Mindi. "Maybe they're celebrating a miracle," came the reply.

About the Authors

Ruth Seligman is a veteran reporter and editor.

Jonathan Mark is associate editor of the New York Jewish Week, where his work was awarded the New York Press Association's "Writer of the Year" and "Best Column: Creative Nonfiction." He is the coauthor, with Dr. Ruth Westheimer, of *Heavenly Sex* (NYU Press).

Jonathan and Ruth (Ruchy) are the very honored parents of Sara Noa Nechama, Rebecca Yona Moriah and Zev Mordechai.

Rabbi Tsvi Blanchard is the Director of Organizational Development at the National Jewish Center for Learning and Leadership (CLAL). Rabbi Blanchard has been a professor of philosophy, the director of the Ida Crown Jewish Academy in Chicago and a practicing clinical and organizational psychologist. In addition to his work in philosophy, social theory and Jewish texts, Rabbi Blanchard has written stories and parables that have been widely anthologized. His recent publications include *How Stories Heal* and *After Eden: The Search for the Holy in a Consumer Society*. He and his wife, Naomi, are the parents of five daughters, Deena, Tali, Tamar, Elana, and Elisheva.